200

KANSAS SCHOOL OF RELIGION
University of Kansas
1300 Oread Avenue
LAWRENCE, KANSAS 66044

D1221620

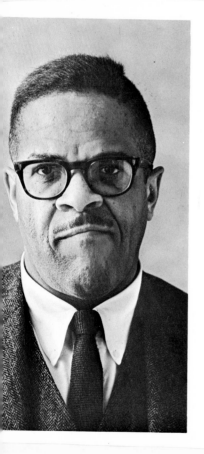

Nathan A. Scott, Jr. is professor of theology and literature in the Divinity School of the University of Chicago and holds a professorship in the University's Department of English. Born in Cleveland in 1925, he is a graduate of the University of Michigan (A.B., 1944), Union Theological Seminary (B.D., 1946), and Columbia University (Ph.D., 1949). From 1948 to 1955 he taught at Howard University where he directed the General Education Program in the Humanities. Mr. Scott is a priest of the Episcopal Church and serves as Canon Theologian of the Cathedral of St. James in Chicago. He is co-editor of The Journal of Religion. *A Fellow of the School of Letters of Indiana University, Mr. Scott holds honorary degrees from Ripon College, Wittenberg University, the Philadelphia Divinity School, and the General Theological Seminary. He is the author of numerous works in literary criticism, including* Modern Literature and the Religious Frontier, Albert Camus, Samuel Beckett, The Broken Center, *and* Craters of the Spirit: Studies in the Modern Novel. *Among books he has edited are* The New Orpheus: Essays Toward a Christian Poetic, The Climate of Faith in Modern Literature, *and* Adversity and Grace: Studies in Recent American Literature.

Negative Capability

KANSAS SCHOOL OF RELIGION
University of Kansas
1300 Oread Avenue
LAWRENCE, KANSAS 66044

KANSAS SCHOOL OF RELIGION
University of Kansas
1300 Oread Avenue
LAWRENCE, KANSAS 66044

Also by Nathan A. Scott, Jr.

Rehearsals of Discomposure: Alienation and Reconciliation in Modern Literature (1952)

Modern Literature and the Religious Frontier (1958)

Albert Camus (1962)

Reinhold Niebuhr (1963)

Samuel Beckett (1965)

The Broken Center: Studies in the Theological Horizon of Modern Literature (1966)

Ernest Hemingway (1966)

Craters of the Spirit: Studies in the Modern Novel (1968)

Edited by Nathan A. Scott, Jr.

The Tragic Vision and the Christian Faith (1957)

The New Orpheus: Essays Toward a Christian Poetic (1964)

The Climate of Faith in Modern Literature (1964)

Man in the Modern Theatre (1965)

Four Ways of Modern Poetry (1965)

Forms of Extremity in the Modern Novel (1965)

The Modern Vision of Death (1967)

Adversity and Grace: Studies in Recent American Literature (1968)

New Haven and London, Yale University Press

Nathan A. Scott, Jr. NEGATIVE
CAPABILITY Studies in the
New Literature and the Religious Situation

P N 49 . S34

KANSAS SCHOOL OF RELIGION
University of Kansas
1300 Oread Avenue
LAWRENCE, KANSAS 66044

Literature, modern -hist. & criticism
religion and literature

Copyright © 1969 by Yale University.
All rights reserved. This book may not be
reproduced, in whole or in part, in any form
(except by reviewers for the public press),
without written permission from the publishers.

Library of Congress catalog card number: 69–15459
Designed by Sally Sullivan,
set in Linotype Palatino type,
by Connecticut Printers, Inc., Hartford, Connecticut,
and printed in the United States of America by
The Carl Purington Rollins Printing-Office
of the Yale University Press.
Distributed in Great Britain, Europe, Asia, and
Africa by Yale University Press Ltd., London; in
Canada by McGill University Press, Montreal; and
in Latin America by Centro Interamericano de Libros
Académicos, Mexico City.

To Joseph Sittler—
and to Joseph Haroutunian, in memoriam

Contents

Preface

In December of 1817 John Keats's adored brothers George and Tom were in Devonshire, whence Tom, the youngest, now unmistakably tuberculous, had been taken in the hope that there the climate might allow him a comfortable winter. Keats was himself living in the little country village of Hampstead, just four miles beyond the northern suburbs of London. On Sunday the 21st he wrote a letter to his brothers, full of news about those with whom he had recently drunk and dined and about his general comings and goings. In the course of this lively calendar of social activity he speaks of having walked back on the previous evening to Hampstead from a Christmas pantomime in London in the company of his good friends and neighbors Charles Armitage Brown and Charles Wentworth Dilke.

Dilke—who, though then holding a post in the Navy Pay Office, was launching for himself what was to be a long and successful career as essayist and editor—had not only won Keats's affection as a friend but also commanded a solid respect, for his strenuous intelligence and seriousness of literary purpose. William Godwin was, of course, the reigning intellectual presence at the time, among young radicals in London; and Dilke was intensely caught up in the excitement generated by Godwin's anarchism. Indeed, he was a man so organized inwardly that, as Keats later realized, he could not even "feel he [had] . . . a personal identity unless he [had]. . . made up his mind about everything," and one suspects that Keats may well have been prepared to say of him as he remarked of Coleridge in his letter (of 21st December, 1817) to his brothers, that Dilke was incapable of *"remaining content with half-knowledge."*

So, given Dilke's habit of espousing his favorite opinions with a great vigorousness, one imagines that on this Saturday night, as he and Brown and Keats walked back from London to Hampstead, he was flailing about with his customary energy, certain of the good-humored tolerance of his friends. They were having, says Keats, *"not a dispute but a disquisition."* He also says (in his letter to George and Tom) that, as it proceeded—with Dilke no doubt taking the larger part—*"several things dove-tailed in my mind, and at once it struck me what quality went to form a Man of Achievement, especially in Literature. . . . I mean* Negative Capability, *that is, when a man is capable of being in uncertainties, mysteries, doubts, without any irritable reaching after fact and reason."*

Now Charles Dilke—this young *"Godwin methodist,"* as Keats called him—was one, it is to be borne in mind, of whom Keats on one occasion felt moved to say that he would *"never come at a truth so long as he lives; because he is always trying at it."* Which was in effect for him to posit as characteristic of his friend just that *"irritable reaching after fact and reason"* of which he took Coleridge to be the period's great exemplar. For Dilke, in other words, life was so real and so earnest that the fibers of his mind were tightened to the point of being virtually tied in a knot; and thus, like an athlete whose excess of training blocks the free flow of energy, Keats felt that his good friend, in whom so much of lightness and buoyancy had been subdued by exertion, might never really come by truth at all, so arduously was he trying at it. It was natural, therefore, in the presence of one for whom life was all *"straining at a moveless latch,"* that he should, by a kind of reflex, have been put in mind of the possibility that what

Preface

is deepest in the human mystery gives way only before a Negative Capability—which Keats, it would appear, did not conceive to be merely an abdication of intellectual enterprise; rather, such a Capability did for him, it seems, entail an intention to make room in the life of the mind for the kind of attitude that prompted Blake's brusque imperative, "Damn braces, bless relaxes." For to feel the full force of "the burthen of the mystery" is to know the absurdity of going through the world like a clenched fist, as though that mystery could simply be battered open or as though the truth that brings joy and gladness to the heart only awaits our grabbing it. Thus Keats wanted to keep in view the possibility that—as Heidegger would say—the "advent" of Being must be waited for, patiently and with no irritable trying at it, in a spirit of meditative openness to the full amplitude of the world. Heidegger's term is not "Negative Capability" but Gelassenheit—which means that spirit of disponibilité before What-Is which permits us simply to let things be in whatever may be their uncertainty and their mystery. When we reach that point where the attempt at bringing the world to heel is given up, when we consent to wait for the advent of Being and to be content with half knowledge, we do so because of some faith, however obscure and inchoate, that we too shall make the discovery of Saul Bellow's Augie March—who has a consuming passion to find the "axial lines" of life and who at last, after many adventures, discovers that, as he says, "When striving stops, there they [the axial lines] are as a gift."

Now the proposal that that quality making for great achievement in literature is a Negative Capability, which permits the imagination's "being in uncertainties, mysteries, doubts," is one of the great testimonies of modern spirituality, and one on which, over a long stretch of time, we have all helped to confer a well-nigh scriptural status. Yet, as we look back upon the classic canon of modern literature, it now appears to be far less informed by Negative Capability than much of the literature that today seems to be peculiarly an expres-

sion of the immediate present. For to look at Yeats, Eliot, Lawrence, Kafka, Joyce, and Brecht is to face writers who had a great "rage for order" and who were profoundly committed to a search for myths and metaphysics whereby the uncertainties, mysteries, doubts of modern experience might be allayed, or at least reduced to a tolerable manageability by the imagination; and it is just the remarkable innovativeness and audacity which they displayed in this search that makes them incarnate so strikingly the very idea of modernity. But today we do, indeed, find ourselves in a period in which the primary quality of the "men of achievement"—of a Beckett, a Robbe-Grillet, a Grass, a Burroughs, a Godard—appears to be a Negative Capability, for they represent, generally, a firm disinclination to transfigure or to try to subdue or resolve what is recalcitrantly indeterminate and ambiguous in the human scene of our time; they do not reach irritably after any great counterpoise to chaos. It seems to me that it is in this that their difference from traditionalist modernism chiefly consists, making a kind of measure of the distance we travel when we move from "the generation of 1914" and their immediate heirs into the spiritual atmosphere distinctively characteristic of our contemporary situation. And it is an intention to remark this difference that lies behind a good part of what I have to say in this book.

The fifth essay I am reprinting from an earlier book (Modern Literature and the Religious Frontier, 1958) which has for some time been out of print and which will not be reissued. The material in the second and third essays formed the basis for the Cole Lectures at Vanderbilt University in the Spring of 1968; and it is an occasion of pleasure for me to be able here to record my gratitude for having been invited to occupy this distinguished platform. I am glad also to record here my very great appreciation of courtesies generously extended to me while I was in Nashville by friends on the Vanderbilt campus.

This book is dedicated to two of my colleagues in the Uni-

Preface

versity of Chicago whose comradeship in all our common tasks in the Divinity School I have greatly treasured over many years, and whose friendship, as it has extended far beyond professional life and embraced our wives and families, has been a constant joy and encouragement.

Chicago   N. A. S., JR.
April, 1968

My friend Joseph Haroutunian died quite suddenly on the fifteenth day of November 1968, and thus, since the above lines were written, it has been necessary for me sadly to alter the Dedication page, making the inscription to him a memorial.

Acknowledgments

"L'Actuelle—*The primary Norm of Our Period-Style*" *was first published (as "The New Mystique of* L'Actuelle: *A View of Cinema in Its Relation to Our Period-Style")* in Man and the Movies, *ed. W. R. Robinson (Baton Rouge, Louisiana State University Press, 1967) and it is included here with the permission of the editor and the publisher.*

"The 'Conscience' of the New Literature" also appears in a volume of essays honoring the late Frederick J. Hoffman, edited by John B. Vickery (Baton Rouge, Louisiana State University Press, 1968).

"Poetry and Prayer" was first published in Thought *(41 no. 160, Spring 1966) and it is reissued here with the permission of Joseph E. O'Neill, S.J., the editor, and the Fordham University Press.*

"Criticism and Theology—The Terms of the Engagement" was originally prepared for the English Institute's Conference on "The Peripheries of Literature" at Columbia University in 1956. It was first published (as "The Collaboration of Vision in the Poetic Act") in Cross Currents *(Spring 1957) and* The Christian Scholar *(December 1957) and was then issued in the English Institute's volume for 1957,* Literature and Belief, *ed. M. H. Abrams (New York, Columbia University Press, 1958). It also formed a part of my book,* Modern Literature and the Religious Frontier *(New York, Harper & Bros., 1958).*

"On the Place of Litterae Humaniores *in the Curriculum of*

Acknowledgments

Theological Studies" was first published (as "Theology and the Literary Imagination") in Adversity and Grace: Studies in Recent American Literature, ed. Nathan A. Scott, Jr. (Chicago, University of Chicago Press, 1968). It is included here by permission of the University of Chicago Press.

Negative Capability

Chapter One L'ACTUELLE—
THE PRIMARY NORM
OF OUR PERIOD-STYLE

I am unable—and I am unaware of anyone else who is able—
to certify the account that Professor Marshall McLuhan of the
University of Toronto (and Fordham University) is giving us
of the profound mutations that are taking place today in the
character of our culture and in the constitution of humankind.
Indeed, the very radical judgment that he is proposing of the
revolutionary "extensions of man" by the new technology of
an electronic age is doubtless marked in some measure by the
afflatus of the seer and the artist, and does to that extent perhaps invite something like an aesthetic response rather than
the objective measurements of empirical science. Surely the
strongest impression that one carries away from such books
as *The Gutenberg Galaxy* and *Understanding Media* is that of
an enormously intelligent (and somewhat cranky) man whose
zany and boundlessly undespairing enthusiasm for all the ico-
nography and gadgetry of a technocratic civilization betokens
what on his part has been an essentially aesthetic response,
of delight and approval, to the novelties created by the electrical media.

But, whether Mr. McLuhan is taken in his capacity as so-
ciologist of culture or as visionary, what he is saying today is
commanding a good deal of attention and offers one of the more
interesting new perspectives from which to survey the landscape of our time. His fundamental contention is that the
whole slant and texture of human sensibility in any age are

determined by the media which the culture employs for the delivery of information. From the Renaissance to the dawn of the contemporary period, the reigning dispensation in the Western world was that of Gutenberg, whose invention of movable type established the basic terms within which reality was perceived by "alphabetic man." That is to say, the rise of a civilization based upon the wide diffusion of the printed word carried, as its major correlate, the development of an ocular sensibility, for the primary cultural reality was that of letters consecutively arranged across a page—and this in turn made for radical change in the style of man's self-interpretation and metaphysical vision. Historicity could now, for example, begin to be a part of the experienced human reality, for the cyclical categories of older mythical perspectives had now to be replaced by linear categories that more nicely comported with the linear structure of the printed page. Not only was the sense of time thus affected, but so, too, was the sense of space. The fixity of the reader's position in relation to the printed page encouraged exploration of perspective in the visual arts, encouraged visual exploration of the multidimensionality of spatial experience, and experiments in chronological montage in narrative literature. And Mr. McLuhan is marvelously adept in suggesting the incalculable social, political, and religious transformations that were a part of the galaxy whose center was formed by Gutenberg's innovation.

The Age of Writing, in his version of modern history, is now a thing of the past, however, and we today belong to the emerging species of "postliterate man," for reality is being codified in a new way. The culture of the book, of the printed page, is being replaced by a new vision of the world based on the grammar and syntax of the electronic image. Mr. McLuhan is therefore announcing the death of "typographic" man. For, ever since the invention of telegraphy, the old eye culture has been in process of being displaced by a polity whose essential logic is an affair of new media, of electronic media, which lead men to experience reality in a new way. Thus the old social

The Primary Norm of Our Period-Style

and art forms that were based in a print culture are slipping into desuetude; a new sensibility is being born. There is, for example, that early and widely known canvas by Picasso, done about 1912, which simply pictures a violin; it is one of the classic expressions of Cubist idiom, and its manifest intention is to eternalize in a single instant all the various possible impressions and views that we might have of a violin—from all possible angles—so that every imaginable perspective might be encompassed at once. Mr. McLuhan would be inclined, one imagines, to take this canvas as a fine instance of the electronic image, for the electrical principle is one of instantaneousness and speed. So the grammar of Cubism—with its emphasis on *simultanéité*, on instant sensory awareness of the whole, on what Mr. McLuhan calls the "total field"—offered an early illustration in the visual art of our century of what the grammar of an electronic culture might be like. But, in order to achieve its fascinating interplay of volumes and planes, a Cubist canvas had to sacrifice that illusion of the third dimension which had been so much a part of the painter's central aim since the Renaissance; and thus, in still another particular, the work of such men as Braque, Derain, Juan Gris, and the early Picasso tended to point toward the kind of general direction that art might be expected to take in an electronic age. For the depthlessness of a Cubist canvas seems presciently to augur for Mr. McLuhan that general disappearance of the dimension of depth which follows after the cultural media are once touched by the electrical principle. Depth orientations in painting, as in literature and all the other arts, had their real roots in the culture of alphabetic man, the man who fed his mind and spirit by solitarily reading portable books and whose isolation from his fellows in turn bred in him the habit of preoccupation with inwardness, with depth, with the "mountains" of the soul— "cliffs of fall/Frightful, sheer, no-man-fathomed."[1] Which is

1. *Poems of Gerard Manley Hopkins*, ed. Robert Bridges, 2d ed. (London and New York, Oxford University Press, 1938), no. 41, p. 62.

5

to say, in Mr. McLuhan's patois, that the great media in the Age of Gutenberg were "hot": whereas today, deep in our electrical age, they are "cool"; for, with depth no longer a primary dimension of experience, the work of art, for example, need not itself any longer be an instrument of phenomenology, a vehicle of man's self-exploration. Indeed, it can now once again be simply an object, and, the horizons of the artist's world being defined by the *désacralisé*, his fundamental work takes on the character of a kind of "research" (into the sheer plasticity of his medium) which is far "closer to the spirit of science than of art in the old-fashioned sense."[2]

Mr. McLuhan's writing, like the electronic images of which he is so fond, gyrates off in so many directions at once and he so dislikes making a clean, direct statement about anything at all that it is extremely difficult to fashion a detailed synopsis of his basic argument; but something like my rough summary may approximate that argument, even if only partially. And his hypothesis, for all of its brilliantly erratic one-sidedness, has at least the merit of confirming in us our tendency to feel the cultural atmosphere of the present as something new and strange. Indeed, it is surely so, in our own late season, that we do begin intermittently to feel a strange sense of disorientation, of belonging already perhaps to the first generation of post-modern people, in a period whose most authentic expressions appear to be found no longer in Hindemith and Bartok but in John Cage and Karlheinz Stockhausen and Milton Babbitt, not in Rouault and Matisse but in Ellsworth Kelley and Frank Stella, not in Malraux and Faulkner but in Beckett and Robbe-Grillet, not in F. R. Leavis and Lionel Trilling but in Maurice Blanchot and Roland Barthes, not in Whitehead and Heidegger but in Wittgenstein and Merleau-Ponty. It is a new scene that we look out upon, and one for which we have not yet even begun to find any comprehensive definition.

Undoubtedly, a part of the response which it is natural for us to make was expressed a few years ago by Lionel Trilling,

2. Susan Sontag, *Against Interpretation* (New York, Farrar, Straus & Giroux, 1966), p. 297.

The Primary Norm of Our Period-Style

in an essay that he called "The Fate of Pleasure."[3] In a tone somewhat of dismayed surprise that this should in fact have for so long been the case, Mr. Trilling remarked how firmly "our contemporary aesthetic culture" is committed to an antihedonist position, to a "diminished status . . . [for] the principle of pleasure"—and this as a consequence, he maintained, of the polemical intention of our literature and art to puncture the "specious good." In the tradition of modern literature, Mr. Trilling uses Dostoevski's *Notes from Underground* and Ivan Karamazov's story of the Grand Inquisitor as his archetypes, and they come, of course, pat to his purpose. Yet the particular cast of their antihedonism, though representative of the classic modern style, is something different, one feels, from what we face in the characteristic art of the present time. For in Dostoevski—as in Kafka, Rouault, Schönberg, and so many of the other great artists who incarnate the period-style of the modern movement—the antihedonist position is not so much an affair of artistic form itself as it is an affair of that account of human existence of which the writer or the painter or musician makes his art a vehicle. The lovemaking of K. and Frieda in *The Castle*, the prostitutes and pariahs of Rouault's *Miserere* series, and the haunting dissonances of Alban Berg's *Wozzeck* express, to be sure, a positive devaluation of the pleasure principle, but in a clarity of form so absolute as to quicken in us the sensation of great beauty. Here we feel that the antihedonism inheres not so much in the actual life of forms as in a certain estimate of the human enterprise which the artist's formal energy converts into a principle of judgment wherewith to assault a "specious good."

In the immediate environment of our contemporary aesthetic culture, however, the pervasive antihedonism is not an affair of ideology. It does not follow upon a polemical engage-

---

3. Lionel Trilling, "The Fate of Pleasure," *Partisan Review*, 30, no. 3 (Summer 1963), 167–91; republished in Mr. Trilling's Collection, *Beyond Culture: Essays on Literature and Learning* (New York, Viking Press, 1965).

ment with a world of specious good and is not, therefore, simply an affair of the experiential material with which art is informed; instead, it seems rather to grow out of the very life of form itself in our time, and it is here, on this most basic level of things, that the possibility of pleasure seems to be precluded. The new music assaults the ear with a cacophony whose violence is greater even than that which was once felt in the twelve-tone constructions of Schönberg and Webern. The painting of a Barnett Newman or a Kenneth Noland affords no chance to enjoy convergences of perspective, spatial intervals, linear rhythms, and orchestrations of plane and volume such as the tradition, from Raphael to Cézanne, from de La Tour to Matisse and Chagall accustoms us to. And *le roman nouveau* in the hands of a Beckett, a Robbe-Grillet, or a Michel Butor, often seems, in its utter plotlessness and banality, to be only an ingeniously designed test of the reader's capacity to endure extremes of tedium.

Thus the denial of pleasure does indeed appear to be a hallmark of the new avant-garde. But if on one level Mr. Trilling helps us to identify what is characteristic of contemporary idioms, it is, I suspect, on a somewhat deeper level that Mr. McLuhan—or what one can piece together of the implications of his thought—helps us toward a proper definition. For the sensation of *dis*pleasure that we are given by the new forms of art is very probably a consequence of the extent to which they have ascetically forsworn the dimension of depth. It is no doubt this artfully deliberate superficiality of the Muse— under the charm perhaps of the electronic image—that puts us off.

In short, disquisitions on the fate of pleasure, though they may move into the general region of what is problematic in our aesthetic transactions today, do not, finally, take us far enough; for what is most basically frustrating in the new art of the present time is its radical depthlessness, its resolute refusal of what Alain Robbe-Grillet may nominate on the day after tomorrow the Anthropocentric Fallacy. Susanne Langer

8

The Primary Norm of Our Period-Style

tells us in her great book, *Feeling and Form*, that the natural function of art is to create "forms symbolic of human feeling," but ours, today, is an art that is determined not to create forms symbolic of *our* feeling. Indeed, John Cage, one of the chief American spokesmen for the new avant-garde in music, believes that the sounds of music should simply "be themselves rather than . . . expressions of human sentiments."[4] So, instead of articulating the morphology of man's affective life, instead of analogically expressing the tensions and resolutions that make up the patterns of human sentience, a musical composition will simply present sounds—not sounds going anywhere or moving through a rhythmically ordered sequence to any sort of climax and thus satisfying expectations aroused by the musical experience, not sounds related to one another by any sort of human logic, but simply sounds, in the sheer thereness of their acousticality. Mr. Cage says, "Wherever we are, what we hear is mostly noise. When we ignore it, it disturbs us. When we listen to it, we find it fascinating."[5] The making of music, he maintains, is simply the "organization of sound," the organization of noise, which is precisely what the music of Christian Wolff, Morton Feldman, and Earle Brown seems to be. The principal concern, as Mr. Wolff says, is for "a kind of objectivity, almost anonymity—sound come into its own."[6] And it is a wonderfully exact formula for the kind of project to which he and his friends are committed— sound come into its own, a music whose most striking feature in its radical depthlessness.

The spiritual depthlessness that is so noticeably characteristic of the style being brought into existence by the new music is by no means, however, an isolated phenomenon in contemporary artistic life; it is an equally striking feature of the archi-

4. John Cage, *Silence* (Middletown, Conn., Wesleyan University Press, 1961), p. 10.
5. Ibid., p. 3
6. Christian Wolff's essay, "New and Electronic Music," quoted in Cage, p. 68.

9

tectural movement of which, say, Mies van der Rohe is a major exemplar. And the movement in recent painting with which we associate the New York School exhibits the same quality. As John Cage wants the sounds of his music to be just there, as sounds come into their own—so Mies wants his Chicago apartment-skyscrapers to be simply skeletons of steel and glass; and a painter like the late Franz Kline wanted many of his canvases to be simply large white fields bearing broad strokes of black: sound, glass and steel, primed canvas and black paint—nothing more, only the sheer thereness of the raw materials, in their unhumanized facticity.

It is in the new *alittérature*, however, that this whole style of sensibility finds perhaps its most candid and resolute expressions, and here the chief strategist is the French novelist-critic Alain Robbe-Grillet. It is undoubtedly the case that such writers as Samuel Beckett, Nathalie Sarraute, Jean Cayrol, Claude Simon, Michel Butor, and M. Robbe-Grillet do not, in all respects, belong under the same umbrella, for their stylistic and narrative procedures manifest a very considerable diversity of aim and stratagem. But, in at least one important particular, they represent a unitary emphasis: in their conviction that narrative literature must be purged of the old "stories," the old structures of plot and character, the old eloquence. They have an equal disdain for the old "anthropomorphism" —for what M. Robbe-Grillet quite explicitly calls "the old myths of 'depth.' "[7] So they dispense with what Claude Simon disapprovingly speaks of as "la merveilleuse illusion," for they believe that the order which the traditional verisimilitudes of prose fiction impose on experience does in fact falsify the existential reality. The great thing, they believe, is, as M. Robbe-Grillet says, "to look at the world which surrounds [us] with entirely unprejudiced eyes." For it is only in this way that its reality can be taken into account, since the locus of that reality is not in the various traditional significations of

7. Alain Robbe-Grillet, *For a New Novel: Essays on Fiction*, trans. Richard Howard (New York, Grove Press, 1965), p. 23.

The Primary Norm of Our Period-Style

the literary imagination but is rather simply in the world's presence: "defying the noisy pack of our animistic or protective adjectives, things *are there*."[8] In a time that "has renounced the omnipotence of the person" and the old "cult of the 'human,' "[9] the principal function of literature must be that of trapping us into a kind of radical amazement at the simple thereness of the world and at the stubbornness with which, in its brute factuality, it resists all our traditional habits of ordering and apprehension. Our writers will become *chosistes*, connoisseurs of *things*, for "the world is neither significant nor absurd. It [simply] is."[10] M. Robbe-Grillet, who is, if nothing else, consistent, develops this mystique of *l'actuelle* more radically than anyone else, producing a fiction from which the human presence has been most rigorously expunged, in which the single subject matter is formed by the novelist's descriptions of the angles, planes, and surfaces of the world—its streets and houses and skies and various other appurtenances. In this way he hopes to create *le roman objectif*.

Now the program which Alain Robbe-Grillet is proposing for the new literature, in the great stringency of its emphasis, has the effect of casting into even higher relief a predominant tendency governing the central movement in the artistic culture of the present time. For, whether we turn to architecture, to painting, to music, or to literature, what is noticeable in the new sensibility is its impatience with "the old myth of 'depth' " and its eagerness to walk "barefoot into reality."[11] A musical composition does not create "forms symbolic of human feeling" but is simply so much organized sound— come into its own. A public building is not visibly in any way a celebration of our common *humanitas* but is simply a structure of concrete or steel. A painting does not "mean" anything extrinsic to itself but is simply so much paint on a cer-

---

8. Ibid., p. 19.
9. Ibid., p. 29.
10. Ibid., p. 19.
11. Wallace Stevens, "Large Red Man Reading," *The Collected Poems* (New York, Alfred A. Knopf, 1954), p. 423.

11

tain area of canvas. A poem is "not ideas about the thing but the thing itself."[12] Everywhere the feeling seems to be that, "instead of making everything an object for the self, the mind must efface itself before reality, or plunge into the density of an exterior world, dispersing itself in a milieu which exceeds it and which it has not made."[13] The sovereign principle seems now to arise out of a new mystique of *l'actuelle.*

Our playwrights having thus discarded the old, well-made structures of beginning-middle-and-end and our poets wanting their poems to *be* rather than *mean* and our novelists being unwilling any longer to tell stories, we are often at the point of wanting querulously to complain about how boring the new literature is. The charge is frequently heard, of course, that the antiseptic purity of much of contemporary architecture puts one in mind of some anonymous public utility—a garage or a warehouse—even when it is a residential apartment building or a center of collegiate studies; the most ardent devotees of the new music will occasionally admit that it is a screeching, screaking vociferation; and the sense of defraudment that is provoked in the galleries devoted to the new painting and sculpture is, of course, a staple of both popular and sophisticated humor. Most of us move along older tracks of perception and taste, and the difficulty we have in following contemporary artists in their attempt to achieve a more radical penetration of *l'actuelle* brings to mind that ironic clause in T. S. Eliot's *Burnt Norton,* "human kind/Cannot bear very much reality."

Indeed, even the movies (long our last refuge from the rigors of modern art) begin to be an extraordinarily difficult and complex form of expression. In the hands of many of the great new artists of the medium—Michelangelo Antonioni, Federico Fellini, Jean-Luc Godard, Alain Resnais—cinema, too,

12. Wallace Stevens, "Not Ideas about the Thing but the Thing Itself," ibid., p. 534.
13. J. Hillis Miller, *Poets of Reality* (Cambridge, Mass., [Belknap Press] Harvard University Press, 1965), pp. 7–8. It is Professor Miller's citations that have put me in mind of the passages of Stevens that are quoted above.

The Primary Norm of Our Period-Style

often seems to be committed to something of the same sort of effort being generally undertaken by much of contemporary art. That gifted young American critic, the late Robert Warshow, objecting to the enthusiasm which leads the *cinéaste* to say, "It is not the *movies* I go to see; it is art," once replied,

> I have gone to the movies constantly, and at times almost compulsively, for most of my life. I should be embarrassed to attempt an estimate of how many movies I have seen and how many hours they have consumed. At the same time, I have had enough serious interest in the products of the "higher" arts to be very sharply aware that the impulse which leads me to a Humphrey Bogart movie has little in common with the impulse which leads me to the novels of Henry James or the poetry of T. S. Eliot. That there is a connection is not adequately summed up in the statement that the Bogart movie and the Eliot poem are both forms of art.[14]

These lines were written in 1954, a few months before Robert Warshow's untimely death, and they do not express, one feels, the kind of lucidity which gave such high interest to much of his writing on films. For the attitude conveyed here, if consistently adhered to, could hardly have made for an adequate response to the best work of William Wyler, George Stevens, John Huston, and Alfred Hitchcock; of Renoir, Carné and Duvivier; of David Lean and Carol Reed; of De Sica and Rossellini. Yet in 1954 an intelligent young American critic could still find it possible to view contemporary cinema as insufficiently serious to compete directly for the same kind of attention that cultivated people in our time give to literature and the other arts—and possible perhaps because in some measure he still belonged to what Parker Tyler calls "the eyewitness

14. Robert Warshow, *The Immediate Experience*, ed. Sherry Abel (Garden City, Doubleday, 1962), p. 27. This passage is from the Author's Preface which originally formed a Statement of Project submitted, with an application for a fellowship, to the Guggenheim Foundation in October of 1954.

era in film fiction,"[15] the period when the predominant film style still found its ultimate source in the ideal of film as documentary, as an eyewitness record of verifiable reality.

Were he alive today, however, it is nearly inconceivable, dedicated as he was to "the tradition of the new," that Warshow would want to insist so firmly on the generic incommensurateness between a serious work of literary art and one of the more characteristic expressions of recent cinema, for the most interesting films of the last ten or fifteen years are very deeply stamped by the new film maker's intention to be an *auteur*. By "auteur" the theoreticians of *Les Cahiers du Cinéma* mean *le directeur par excellence*—the director who is so thoroughly the impresario of the entire creative process resulting in the completed film that he is indeed its primary cause and author, having chosen his subject, superintended the preparation of his script, selected his cast and cameramen, and controlled all the editing; in fact, having exercised a decisive hand in every phase of the total sequence of actions whereby a film is made. The auteur is the master of the entire process of film creation, who uses his work as a vehicle to express a personal vision of the world. And this is indeed the role that is played today by a Truffaut, an Antonioni, a Resnais (as in an earlier time by a Welles or a Cocteau).

Like the new dramatists and novelists, the auteur often takes only a very slight interest in "stories." The principal focus of his interest lies rather in the *mise en scène*, in the mood and tonality of moments which, by dint of audacious technical maneuvers—in photography or the use of sound or editing—can be made to become epiphanies (in something like the sense established by Joyce for prose fiction). So the model in one's mind of an auteur's film is one that has forsworn most of the conventional techniques of cinematic narration. What the director conceives his main task to be is not the exposition of a traditional linear plot but the manipulation of the forms and movements of screen images; and thus the

15. Parker Tyler, *The Three Faces of the Film* (New York, Thomas Yoseloff, 1960), pp. 23–35.

The Primary Norm of Our Period-Style

temporality of this cinema is one which has lost the uninterrupted continuity of concrete, objective time. The new filmmaker, characteristically, has little interest in developing consecutive sequences of events; for him the grammar of film has but a single tense—and the time dimension of cinematic happenings is the radical present. So the auteur tends to splice scenes together in ways that rob the spectator of the kinds of yardsticks that have traditionally been provided for his equanimity. What the director wants to do is not to carry the spectator comfortably along through the various logical stages of a linear narrative but, rather, to involve him deeply in the special quality of a given instant, and then of another and another; and he assumes that the spectator's intelligence is agile enough to make the necessary connections. The auteur specializes in the unexpected, the contradictory, in seeming irrelevancy. Things are shifting, fragmentary, evanescent, because reality is felt to be dynamic and volatile; and the world is exhibited as a place of sudden and mysterious landmarks. Cinematic structure is conceived to be something like what Jacques Guicharnaud finds to be the structure of a novel by Claude Simon —a structure, that is,

> rather similar to a cloud, formed by the wind, which at a given moment takes on a recognizable—or at least noticeable—shape, then changes into another, and perhaps still another, finally becoming shapeless, lost in the greyness of a clouded sky. Just as, in the fluid, heterogeneous and constantly moving substance of life, there forms a kind of ephemeral coagulation, a vague nucleus distinguishable for a short while, yet without any break in continuity with the rest.[16]

The film itself, in other words, is the primary reality. This is what the director wants us to remember that we are watching, a film and nothing but a film: the emphasis is on spectacle and sound, on the way things look and feel; what is striven for

16. Jacques Guicharnaud, "Remembrance of Things Passing: Claude Simon," *Yale French Studies*, no. 24 (Summer 1959), p. 103.

is an art of appearances whose informing spirit is that of a mystique of *l'actuelle.*

It is, I say, very much this general sort of image that one carries in one's mind of the kind of cinema being produced by the most gifted and the most characteristic film makers of the present time; and, were Robert Warshow alive today, he would, I suspect, feel compelled to admit that this is a cinema the style of whose aesthetic pretensions is indeed very much of a piece with the way in which the serious art of our time generally establishes its claims upon us.

The particular film that does, I suppose, for me, more nearly than any other, stand as a kind of emblem of the new period is Alain Resnais' remarkable production of 1961, *L'Année dernière à Marienbad* (the scenario for which was prepared by Alain Robbe-Grillet). Had I to name the half-dozen (or even, the dozen) films of the last ten or fifteen years that have given me the greatest pleasure and that I regard as the most considerable achievements in the medium, there might very probably not be room for *Marienbad* on my list, for my own sense of things makes me doubtful of its meriting the rank that I would reserve, say, for Robert Bresson's *Le Journal d'un Curé de Campagne,* for Fellini's *La Strada* and *La Dolce Vita,* for Bergman's *Wild Strawberries* and *The Virgin Spring,* for Truffaut's *Les Quatre Cents Coups,* or for Resnais' own *Hiroshima mon Amour.* But, nevertheless, it is *Marienbad* that first comes to my mind when I begin to think of what is characteristically new and radical in the cinema of our time; it gives the age away, in the sense of presenting in itself a kind of summary of our period-style.

We are taken into a vast baroque hotel, cavernous in its seemingly endless labyrinth of corridors, halls silent and deserted and icy in their elaborately stuccoed and marbled elegance, where, as a neutral and monotonous male voice says (after the credits have been shown), "the sound of advancing footsteps is absorbed by carpets so thick and heavy that nothing can be heard . . . as if the ear itself were very far away . . . from this heavy and empty setting." Here, after the camera

The Primary Norm of Our Period-Style

has roamed through the corridors and galleries of this lugubrious palace, it moves into a faintly lit salon where the elegantly attired guests are stiffly disposed about the room, in chairs all turned in the same direction; it then focuses in on three of these personages, a woman (A) and two men (X and M). The remainder of the film is very largely given over to the pursuit of A by X. X proposes to her that they met last year at Marienbad, that they had an affair there, and he insists that, though something then prevented their going away together, she agreed to meet him here a year hence and promised that, at this time, they would go off with each other. A at first denies the entire recital and asserts that in fact they have never met before at all. But X will not be put off; he insists that they were indeed together a year ago—at Marienbad. He says,

> "You never seemed to be waiting for me—but we kept meeting at each turn of the paths—behind each bush, at the foot of each statue, near each pond. . . . One night, I went up to your room. . . . It was almost summer. . . . I remember that room very well. . . . You were sitting on the edge of the bed, in a kind of robe or bed-jacket. . . . I took you, half by force."

But though for a while A insists that she has never seen him before and that he is inventing the whole tale, gradually she begins to weaken—under the force of his reiterations and his denial that M is really her husband: "Yes. . . . Maybe. . . ."

Meanwhile, as this strange colloquy goes on—always off-screen—the restless camera is forever dwelling upon the decorative details of the great hotel, the gloomy distances spanned by its corridors, its monumental staircases, its imposing colonnades, its sumptuously appointed salons, the grandiloquent spaciousness of its geometrically formal gardens *à la française*. And this camera behaves with great eccentricity. It will shoot the same action over and again, from different angles, sliding away from the persons upstage and then rushing back in upon them; or a shot will change in the middle of a speech, which

17

then continues offscreen during the shot that follows (and the change of shot is likely to be accompanied by the crash of a cymbal); or a shot will go dark and then brighten again, showing the same scene; or the scenes of intense emotion will be overexposed, the screen being flooded with a dazzling white effect.

Indeed, the film is very largely, almost wholly, an affair of the camera alone, for very few words are actually spoken by M. Resnais' actors. What he offers is something chiefly to be seen rather than heard; and what we see are X and A and the various other people in the hotel moving up and down its vast corridors, stiff and icy in the formality of their haute couture, entering salons, closing doors, and, with a kind of ritualistic deliberateness, taking up positions against the background of the baroque decor, as if they were acting out an elegant charade in parody of the International Set. But we learn nothing at all about these people—not even about X and A. A, to be sure, does it seems, bit by bit, come finally to accept X's account of what happened last year at Marienbad; and, at last, they do apparently leave the hotel together. But who is A, really? And who is X? We never find out. And were they together last year at Marienbad? M. Robbe-Grillet peremptorily denies that any previous meeting ever occurred, suggesting that what is involved here is simply a contest of wills which X finally wins, by forcing A to accept his version of things. But M. Resnais, though he offers us the privilege of making whatever we will of the film, asserts that he could never have shot it had he not been convinced that the meeting had actually taken place. The question, of course, as to what really happened last year at Marienbad is very much like the question as to "how many children had Lady Macbeth?" Along this route, no great progress is likely to be made. But at least it can be fairly argued that the man X and the woman A whom we see on the screen are there beheld as people without any past at all: they come from nowhere; they have no backgrounds, no connections, no past and no future; and they exist discarnately, amid the ostentatious magnificence of a great hotel.

The Primary Norm of Our Period-Style

And where is this hotel? Or is it, after all, really a hotel? Is it, as some have supposed, a kind of sanatorium in which X (the psychiatrist) is attempting to assist A toward some fresh repossession of herself? Or is it perhaps that this gloomy palace —like that Second Empire living room in Sartre's *Huis Clos*— is an image of Hell? One cannot be certain, for no story is told of human beings recognizably like ourselves, and the film is not "about" anything at all; it carefully forswears "the old myth of 'depth' " and wants to be simply an end in itself, a pure film, something utterly and absolutely autonomous. So it resists interpretation. In its intransigent objectivism, it offers us simply an art of appearances whose sole purpose is to exhibit the sheer sensuous immediacy of film images—and these are surely among the most captivatingly beautiful images that have ever appeared on the movie screen.

Now there are, of course, many who have a great eagerness to assail the whole style of expression embodied in cinema by *Marienbad*— or in literature by the novels of Robbe-Grillet or the poetry of Charles Olson, or in philosophy by British linguistic analysis, or in painting by the work of Franz Kline and Mark Rothko, or in music by the work of John Cage—as representing a new *trahison des clercs* that threatens a nihilistic subversion of everything humane and elevating in the received traditions of culture. The deliberate depthlessness of a cultural style whose intent is to do nothing more than describe the appearances of the life-world seems to entail a certain foreshortening of things and a certain abdication from the multidimensionality of the real. There is no dearth of angry, irascible traditionalists who are prepared to sound the hue and the cry—of treason.

I have no doubt, of course, but that a partisanship in behalf of "the tradition of the new" which is so ardent as to exempt it from any stringently critical scrutiny must make, in the long run, for a real *trahison*. And being temperamentally more inclined perhaps toward traditionalist sympathies than toward the headiness of avant-gardist enthusiasms, I am most assuredly myself prepared to testify to a very strong sense of

19

L'Actuelle—

much being left out, after hearing the music of Luigi Nono and Morton Feldman and remembering that of Bartok and Hindemith or after looking at the paintings of Newman and Stella and remembering the great ones of Picasso and Matisse or after seeing Fellini's *8½* or Antonioni's *La Notte* and remembering Renoir's *La Grande Illusion* or De Sica's *Shoeshine*. But surely there is something profoundly decadent and obscurantist in that attitude of mind which prompts an outright denunciation of new forms of art because they commit what is presumed to be the great sin of simply being unlike older forms of art. And I suspect that what it is most important for us to do today, before attempting any measurements of the new idioms in accordance with older norms, is to ask what genuinely creative and valuable function it may be which is performed by an art that has rigorously forsworn the dimension of depth for the sake of fidelity to appearances.

It is at this point that I am immediately put in mind of that great old phrase occurring in the sixth-century *Commentary* by Simplicius on Aristotle's *De Caelo*—σώζειν τὰ φαινόμενα, "to save the appearances."[17] For this, one begins to feel, is what it is a major impulse of the most characteristic contemporary art to try to do—to save the appearances, or to do what Goethe told Schiller (in a letter dated February 10, 1798) it is "the better part of human nature" to attempt; namely, to try "to bestow upon the concrete the honor of the idea." From Goethe and Blake to Bergson and D. H. Lawrence there is, of course, a persistent movement of protest in the modern period against what Whitehead (in *Science and the Modern World*) called the Fallacy of Misplaced Concreteness. Whether one turns, say, in philosophic tradition, to Kierkegaard or to Merleau-Ponty, or, in literary tradition, to Hopkins or to Wallace Stevens, one can sense a recurrent anxiety of the modern imag-

17. The phrase has fascinated me ever since I read the discussion of Simplicius occurring in a book published a few years ago by that interesting English thinker, Owen Barfield, which he called *Saving the Appearances* (New York, Harcourt, Brace and World, [Harbinger Books] n.d.).

20

The Primary Norm of Our Period-Style

ination that, in the course of our growing enslavement to the disruptiveness of the analytical passions, we may altogether lose any living contact with the existential reality of the world we actually inhabit—its smells, sounds, sights, and tactilities—becoming entangled, finally, in nothing more than an arid morass of utter abstractions. The great specter that has recurrently haunted many of the most sensitive men of the last two hundred years is that there may eventually come a time when all the richness and amplitude of Creation will simply pass through the eyes of a man into his head and there be turned by the brain into some sort of formula or equation.[18] But this tradition of protest against what Lawrence called "mentalism" has been, by and large, a minority movement, for we are a people so committed to the Idea (and thus to the Will) as not to have been able, except intermittently, really to accept the possibility that the mind might occasionally need to abandon its imperialist ambitions, might need even for a while to consent to be dumb and stupid before reality, in order once again to win access to "the dearest freshness deep down things."

Our generation begins increasingly to fear, however, that the analytical passions, grown swollen and rampant, may, through their demonic ingeniousness, be simply promoting "the vain and desperate fidgetings of the good intention to make hell a better place to live in."[19] A holocaustal glow is descried in the not too distant skies. So, expressing no doubt a deep drive of our age, the contemporary artist wants very much, as it were, to return to the earth, remembering perhaps the word of Hölderlin, that this is indeed where man dwells, at least poetically, "upon the earth." In an age whose abstractions begin to promise death to civilization and to the human

18. My own sentence derives from the sentence in Flannery O'Connor's novel *The Violent Bear It Away*, in which Old Tarwater furiously splutters out the charge against his schoolteacher-nephew, Rayber, that "every living thing that passed through . . . [his] eyes into his head was turned by his brain into a book or a paper or a chart."

19. Erich Heller, *The Disinherited Mind: Essays in Modern German Literature and Thought* (Philadelphia, Dufour and Saifer, 1952), p. 26.

21

spirit and to the very earth itself, the motion that the artist begins now to perform with a new seriousness is a motion of digging away at and recovering those elemental givens of experience in which, as Stevens says, "we awake,/Within the very object that we seek,/Participants of its being."[20] The aim is to see "the very thing and nothing else";[21] the principal search (in painting, music, literature, and the cinema) is for what Goethe called the *Urphänomen*; and, in this way, it is hoped that, by impaling the imagination on the very things of earth themselves, by saving "the appearances," we may save ourselves. It is, I suspect, in some such terms as these that we must finally understand the new mystique in the artistic life of our period, of *l'actuelle*.

The campaign, however, which is generally under way in contemporary art is of a kind that will constantly skirt inanity and innocuousness, if it be not remembered, as Goethe insisted in his *Theory of Colors*, that

> the mere looking at a thing is of no use whatsoever. Looking at a thing gradually merges into contemplation, contemplation into thinking, thinking is establishing connections, and thus it is possible to say that every attentive glance which we cast on the world is [ultimately] an act of theorizing.[22]

The mere looking at a thing is of no use whatsoever; to gaze deeply at any reality is already to be by way of beginning to perform an act of theorizing. This is a profound lesson that has been thoroughly mastered by those artists, even those most radically committed to "the very thing itself," who make the greatest impress upon us, for they are artists—a Benjamin Britten, a Francis Bacon, a Bertolt Brecht, a Robert Lowell, an Ingmar Bergman—who show (as Mr. Trilling rightly predicts they will)[23] that they are "aware of rhetoric, which is to

20. Stevens, "Study of Images I," *Collected Poems*, p. 463.
21. Stevens, "Credences of Summer," ibid., p. 373.
22. Quoted in Erich Heller, p. 19.
23. Lionel Trilling, *The Liberal Imagination* (New York, Viking Press, 1950), p. 290.

say, of the intellectual content of their work." Goethe's lesson is, I suspect, the great lesson that much of contemporary art needs to be learning anew: that strict attention to what the poet Richard Wilbur calls the "things of this world"[24] needs finally to lead to a kind of theorizing, a theorizing, as Goethe says, that will be immensely ironic but that will, nevertheless, entail for the artist a kind of double reversal—*away* from the idea to the things themselves but at last *back* to the idea.

This is the way that a Robbe-Grillet needs to take, that a John Cage needs to take, that surely must begin to be taken by the new painters if they are to avoid that absolute impasse towards which they often seem today to be heading. And this is even, I should say, the lesson that our new filmmakers will be having to learn, if the rich promise in much of their work is to find any large fulfillment. Indeed, it is what I take to be the major implication of a now classic essay on contemporary cinema, the piece that the French critic Alexandre Astruc contributed to *L'Écran Français* in 1948 and that he called "Le Caméra Stylo." In likening the camera to a fountain pen, M. Astruc meant to suggest that the cinema is in fact a kind of language, a form of writing:

> By a language, I mean the form in which and through which an artist can express his thoughts, however abstract they may be, or translate his obsessions, just as in an essay or a novel. . . . The film will gradually free itself from the tyranny of the visual, of the image for its own sake, of the immediate anecdote, of the concrete, to become a means of writing as supple and as subtle as that of written language. . . . What interests us in the cinema today is the creation of this language.

Of course, M. Astruc's conception of the camera as a fountain pen with which one writes may now perhaps be seen to have been less a prediction of things immediately to come than a recommendation to film makers of what ought to be

24. See Richard Wilbur, *Things of This World* (New York, Harcourt, Brace, 1956).

23

their intended course. I say that it seems now to have been less a prediction than a recommendation, because, in the intervening years, the reigning principle in so much of avant-garde cinema has continued to be largely an affair of "the tyranny of the visual, of the image for its own sake," of an art of appearances. Yet I am certain that M. Astruc is basically right in believing that the artist of film must also be a rhetorician—as was a Chaplin, a Cocteau, a Renoir; or as is a Bergman, a Tony Richardson, a Fellini in his finest work. Thus I suspect that, for all of its visual beauty, such a film as *L'Année dernière à Marienbad*, in its inordinate fascination with the concrete, more nearly exemplifies what is problematic in cinema today than it charts a course toward larger possibilities of expression. For the concrete begins to take on radical significance only when it can be seen to be leading into the "concrete universal." And this is a route today taken too infrequently.

Chapter Two THE "CONSCIENCE"
OF THE
NEW LITERATURE

Those hucksters who make it a business in our literary life
to sniff out and then to advertise *Tendenz,* whether at the level
of the *Partisan Review* or of our Sunday Supplements, appear,
rather curiously, not to have noticed one interesting development of the last few years. For the increasing commerce between the disciplines of theology and literary criticism has
very largely gone unremarked, outside a relatively small circle. But, though unadvertised and without celebrity, the recent
inclination of these two fields of thought to move toward a
point of convergence makes a significant circumstance of the
present time. It may not constitute what Lionel Trilling would
call a "cultural episode," but it is at least a development which,
if carefully attended to, may have the effect of revealing some
of the emerging landmarks of what Harold Rosenberg calls
"the tradition of the new."

On the side of theology, the enormous prestige which the
modern literary enterprise has come to have may in part perhaps be a consequence of an eagerness to descry some sort of
disguised *preparatio evangelica* amid all the clanging hetero-
doxy of this century's poetry, drama, and fiction. Undoubtedly, what was once called "apologetics" or what we now
speak of as "theology of culture" represents an endeavor
which is to some extent controlled by a desire to disallow the
possibility of any cultural force or movement being untouched
by religious meaning of a positive kind. Most of our younger

25

theologians have, at one time or another, displayed a remarkable expertise in the art of turning up Tillich's "God above God" in cultural materials which were themselves very emphatically committed to secular modes of statement. But, in the transaction they have attempted to negotiate between themselves and the modern artist, the apologetic interest has by far been superseded by the intention to listen to the news the arts can bring us about what the jargon of our period calls the Human Condition.

Very often, one suspects, without being aware of its ancestry, the theological community (under the influence of thinkers like Maritain, Berdyaev, and Tillich) has been guided in its dealings with literature and the arts, perhaps most basically, by an idea which first took hold of the modern imagination in the late eighteenth and early nineteenth centuries, during the high period of the Romantic movement. It is the notion, descending from Lessing and Hegel through Herder to Madame de Staël and Taine, that the great function of art as a cultural institution, and most especially of literary art, is that of providing a very sensitive kind of barometer of the *Zeitgeist*, or of what Taine, in his famous trinity, spoke of as "race," "moment," and "milieu." When the American Protestant theologian, Amos Wilder, tells us that we may find in the literature of the modern period "our best clues to the diagnosis of men's hearts and the deeper movements of the age,"[1] we recognize an emphasis which is often present today in theological analysis of cultural life; and we feel, too, that the Hegelianism of a Taine is not far distant—the sort of sentiment to which Hegel himself gave concise expression when he said in his *Aesthetik*: "Every work of art belongs to its time, its people, and its environment" (*So dann gehört jedes Kunstwerk seiner Zeit, seinem Volke, seiner Umgebung*).

The kind of Hegelian aesthetic of the Time-Spirit which has tended to govern recent theology in its method of approaching imaginative literature has appeared, of course, over a long

1. Amos N. Wilder, *Modern Poetry and the Christian Tradition* (New York, Charles Scribner's Sons, 1952), p. xi.

the New Literature

period to find a very considerable sanction in the general style of the modern writer's pursuit of his vocation. Indeed, the fundamental aim of modernism might be said to have been (if I may lift out of its context a phrase of the English critic, John Holloway) that of "living in the whole present."[2] Or perhaps a phrase of Stephen Spender's is even more apt, for he speaks of the distinctively modern vision in literature as a "vision of the whole."[3] This makes, I believe, for an exact specification, for in the last hundred years or so the literary imagination has been overtaken by a most acute seizure of fascination with our metaphysical poverty, with what Wallace Stevens calls "the spectacle of a new reality." This new reality is, of course, the catastrophic dishabilitation of that "whole/Shebang"[4] which was once considered to be a providentially ordered world. Not only has there disappeared that structure of archaic cosmology which Rudolf Bultmann speaks of as "the three-storied universe,"[5] but so, too, has the whole framework of the *philosophia perennis* suffered an irreversible collapse. Modern mentality simply has not beheld the world, and cannot behold it, as a hierarchy of orders intellectually appropriable by way of a metaphysical ascent through "the degrees of knowledge" to the Divine Principle which reigns at the apex of the whole. For nearly two hundred years we have been in the West an incorrigibly nonmetaphysical people, at least in the sense of being unable—except by way of scholastic tour de force—to construe reality in terms of two realms. The whole procedure whereby it has been natural since the Enlightenment for men to make sense of themselves and their world has been one which has effectively undermined the

2. See John Holloway, *The Colours of Clarity* (London, Routledge & Kegan Paul, 1964), chap. 1.

3. See Stephen Spender, *The Struggle of the Modern* (Berkeley and Los Angeles, University of California Press, 1963), chap. 2 of part II.

4. Wallace Stevens, "The Comedian as the Letter C," *Collected Poems*, p. 37.

5. See Rudolf Bultmann, "New Testament and Mythology," *Kerygma and Myth*, ed. Hans Werner Bartsch, and trans. Reginald H. Fuller (New York, Harper [Torchbooks], 1961), pp. 1–44.

old supposition that progress towards "the really real" moves along an upward path, along some sort of analogical ladder, from the public world of natural and historical phenomena to a spiritual or noumenal world of pure Being. Indeed, all the pre-Kantian certainties of the *fides perennis* have long since disappeared, an occurance which might be said to be the central event of modern history. The linchpin of that entire conceptual scheme is simply gone; though it once carried cogency, it does so no longer, for, as Wallace Stevens phrases it, "A tempest [having] cracked on the theatre," what is now most real is

> The rip
> Of the wind and the glittering . . .
> In the spectacle of a new reality.[6]

In short, as Léon Bloy said many years ago, "Modern man has been brought to bay at the extremity of all things."[7] And, in this severe situation, the literary artist has felt obliged to seek a vision of the whole—or at least the writers whom we now regard as classically incarnating the period-style of modernity are those who risked some comprehensive judgment of the whole present.

"What has happened," declared the late R. P. Blackmur, "[is that] almost the whole job of culture has been dumped on the artist's hands."[8] Judging from the many similar testimonies that have come from virtually all the focal strategists of the modern movement, it would indeed appear to have been felt to be the case that a vast job had been jumped on the writer's hands. In this connection, one could bring forward relevant declarations from so diverse a group of representative figures as Arthur Rimbaud, Matthew Arnold, Henry James, William Butler Yeats, Rainer Maria Rilke, André

6. Stevens, "Repetitions of a Young Captain," *Collected Poems*, p. 306.

7. Quoted in Stanley Romaine Hopper, *The Crisis of Faith* (New York and Nashville, Abingdon-Cokesbury Press, 1944), p. 15.

8. R. P. Blackmur, *The Lion and the Honeycomb* (New York, Harcourt, Brace and World, [Harvest Books], 1955), p. 206.

Breton, Jean-Paul Sartre—but T. S. Eliot's famous testimony, in the review that he published in the *Dial* in 1923 of Joyce's *Ulysses*, makes as good an exhibit as any other. The significant thing is, of course, that, as Eliot undertook to confront and assess Joyce's astonishing accomplishment just a few months after the book's appearance, what he was impressed by above all else was the extent to which Joyce, in using an Homeric paradigm, "in manipulating a continuous parallel between contemporaneity and antiquity," had found "a way of controlling, of ordering, of giving a shape and a significance to the immense panorama of futility and anarchy which is contemporary history." It was, he suggested, such "a step toward making the modern world possible for art" as could be taken only by those who had "won their own discipline in secret and without aid, in a world which offers very little assistance to that end."[9] The implicit assumption was that inherited systems of reference had broken down; that, in order for the spectacle of the new reality to be mastered, the artist had to take on "the whole job of culture," raiding dead tradition for the still viable remnant of meaning, minting out of his own untrammeled inventiveness new world-hypotheses, and so ordering it all as somehow to give a shape and a significance to a world which itself offers very little assistance toward the attainment of a coherent vision of human existence. What was implicitly assumed was that, in a late and difficult time, the artist's natural effort will be that of finding a whole present in which to live and that any vision of the whole which he achieves will have been managed by a discipline won "in secret and without aid."

Despite the brevity of Eliot's early account of the meaning of Joyce's achievement, it is today a classic, and we have long since discerned the marvelous accuracy with which it expressed the modern writer's sense of his own situation and charted the course which he was undertaking. For the people

9. T. S. Eliot, "Ulysses, Order, and Myth," first appeared in the *Dial* (November 1923); reprinted in John W. Aldridge (ed.), *Critiques and Essays on Modern Fiction: 1920–1951* (New York, Ronald Press, 1952).

who incarnate the idea of modernity—the Pound of *Mauberley* and the *Cantos*, the Joyce of *Ulysses*, the Eliot of *The Waste Land*, the Rilke of the *Duino Elegies*, the Pirandello of *Six Characters*, the Yeats of *The Tower* and *The Winding Stair*, the Faulkner of *The Sound and the Fury*—are all artists who felt what Wordsworth called "the weight of all this unintelligible world." Knowing themselves to be disinherited of an effective metaphysical machinery for the ordering of experience, they proceeded to improvise into existence new systems of meaning and faith. Thus, however untouched they may have been by the usages of orthodoxy, there is in their work, we feel, an austere religious grandeur that is an expression of the stringent honesty and courage with which they move through tracts of the spirit left darkened by the recession of older codes and beliefs. It is, indeed, a literature drenched in the passions of metaphysics and theology; and it should be no occasion for surprise that that vanguard in criticism which has undertaken to plot and to explicate the established canon of the modern movement should so frequently have had to enter an area of theological reflection. Nor is it any less strange, given the general shape and tendency of modern literature, that the most alert professional theologians should be deeply drawn, as they have been, to this whole body of art, as a kind of unconsecrated scripture arising out of the innermost chambers of the heart in a straitened age.

Many years ago, early in the first decade of this century, Santayana suggested that literature always reveals a special sort of "piety" or "conscience," for "it cannot long forget, without forfeiting all dignity, that it serves a burdened and perplexed creature."[10] And it might be said that the distinctively modern element in modern literature was in part an affair of the consistency with which the "conscience" of that literature prompted the artist to compete with that "immense panorama of . . . anarchy" of which Eliot spoke in his review

10. George Santayana, *The Life of Reason, 4, Reason in Art* (New York, Charles Scribner's Sons, 1905), p. 84.

of *Ulysses.* Haunted by an "enormous dream of . . . the mortality of [the] gods"[11] and of the consequent disarray of the human City, the literary imagination undertook to find a stay against the confusion in new myths and metaphysics. Whether one turns to Joyce or Mann or Broch, or to Rilke or Yeats or Eliot, one feels that what is being proffered, at bottom, is some vast metaphor or parable about Time and Destiny, about History and the Human Prospect. The *analogia fidei* no longer being available as a way to ultimate affirmation, the modern artist turned then to a new method of reflection, proceeding by way of what might be called the *analogia extremitatis.* If this dialectical route did not yield a new *analogia entis,* at least the radicalism with which the writer spanned the great frontiers of modern experience gave an immense vibrancy and poignance to metaphysical perplexity and had the effect of expressing that peculiar form and pressure which constituted "the very age and body of the time."

Indeed, it is just as we remember the audaciousness and urgency with which the classic literature of our period was competing with reality, it is just as we remember its passion to face into and alter the course of history, that we are bound to be put in mind of how great is now the distance that already separates the contemporary landscape from the modern tradition; it is just here that we begin to sense how deeply literature has already moved into a post-modern phase. One doesn't know quite where to locate the point at which the transition began. Perhaps the search for origins might go back to Rimbaud's fascination with "the voluptuousness of nirvana,"[12] or to Mallarmé's disenchantment with "the literary game," or to Kafka's curious aesthetic of indeterminacy which made his fiction so astonishing when it first began to be widely read thirty years ago. But wherever may be the point which

11. Ihab Hassan, "The Dismemberment of Orpheus: Reflections on Modern Culture, Language and Literature," *The American Scholar,* 32, no. 3 (Summer 1963), p. 463.

12. Marcel Raymond, *From Baudelaire to Surrealism* (New York, Wittenborn, Schultz, 1950), p. 33.

is to be identified as that at which the modern period in literature begins already to be drawing to a close, there is, early on
in Robert Musil's novel *The Man Without Qualities*, a sentence which can now be seen to have been prophetic of the
new turn which the literary imagination was to take in its
post-modern phase. It is the sentence in which Musil tells us
that "no serious attempt will be made to . . . enter into competition with reality." His meaning is that the simple sequen-
tiality of literary narrative—and then, and then, and then—is
no longer a true simulacrum of human experience; however
comforting its illusion of order and necessity may once have
been, the illusion has lost its beguiling power, and both
Musil and his hero Ulrich take it for granted that "everything
has now become non-narrative." The concrete experiential
material of the world, in this very late season, has somehow
become so intractable, so radically contingent, as to make any
attempt of the artist to compete with it not only futile but
inauthentic, and even fraudulent. And he therefore best
"serves a burdened and perplexed creature" by relegating to
the discard as utterly specious the old illusions, the mistaken
supposition that literary art can give "a shape and significance
to the immense panorama of . . . anarchy" which is our present situation. What the conscience of the artist must now require, Musil wants in effect to say, is that the work of art
simply be, in its own tenuous fragmentariness and indeterminacy, an image of the actual world to which man is condemned. In his manifest impatience with the logic of traditional narrative order, it would in fact seem that it was such
an image that he was himself attempting to create in *The Man
Without Qualities;* for, given the "mere anarchy [which] is
loosed upon the world," it is a novel which wants only to provide an illustration of that chaos.

This refusal to compete with reality—which marks what
may well be the central impulse of the post-modern movement
in literature—undoubtedly reaches well back into the nineteenth century, and most especially into those French Romantics who, as Mario Praz says, exalted "the artist who does not

give a material form to his dreams—the poet ecstatic in front of a forever blank page, the musician who listens to the prodigious concerts of his soul without attempting to translate them into notes."[13] "It is romantic," Praz suggests, "to consider concrete expression as a decadence, a contamination,"[14] and this is at least the feeling represented by that French line that runs, crookedly, from Rimbaud through Mallarmé and Valéry to Maurice Blanchot. But there are, of course, still other antecedents of the contemporary refusal of that imperial imagination so typical of classic modernism, which was beautifully described by Yeats when, in a famous phrase, he expressed his desire to hold together reality and justice in a single thought. In, for example, those baffling arabesques of Kafka's, one senses a deep disposition of the artist to forswear that structurally enclosed kind of autonomy which was so much the intention of traditionalist modernism; the ambiguity which this poet of the novel experienced in his encounter with the world was so radical that, far from dreaming of his art as a way of subduing the anarchy and of holding together reality and justice, he could only create a tantalizingly opaque fiction whose meanings were deliberately left unresolved and open. It is a similar procedure that is also noticeable in Gide's *The Counterfeiters*, in Ford Madox Ford's *The Good Soldier*, in Djuna Barnes' *Nightwood*, in Ivy Compton-Burnett's *A House and Its Head*, in Nabokov's *Pale Fire*, in Bellow's *Seize the Day*—a procedure which has the effect of conveying the writer's sense of the world's so far surpassing the framing devices of art as to render both futile and fraudulent the attempt, were he to make it, to enter into any very strenuous competition with reality

Again, a kind of disavowal of modernism's ambitiousness for the large reconstructive effort is to be felt in the fleeting deliquescence and vague, shadowy mistiness so much culti-

13. Mario Praz, *The Romantic Agony*, trans. Angus Davidson (Cleveland and New York, World Publishing Co. [Meridian Books] 1956), p. 15.
14. Ibid.

vated by Virginia Woolf, who proposed, in her much-quoted manifesto of 1919 (on "Modern Fiction"), to "record the atoms as they fall upon the mind in the order in which they fall." This was the only pattern she wanted to trace—"the pattern, however disconnected and incoherent in appearance, which each sight or incident scores upon the consciousness." There is no doubt a fairly straight line leading from the Virginia Woolf of *To the Lighthouse* through the Djuna Barnes of *Nightwood* to the Malcolm Lowry of *Under the Volcano* and the Nathalie Sarraute of *Tropismes*. For these are writers—and the list could be enlarged—who adhere to something like the sort of standard Virginia Woolf was herself embracing. Their characters, for example, as one of Mrs. Woolf's critics has remarked of her own, "are not characters" but are left somehow "unfinished, spreading as the ripples of a lake spread in the sunlight."[15] They give the impression of being unfinished because they have been dissolved into psychological tropisms, into (in Mrs. Woolf's phrase) the "incessant shower of innumerable atoms" that fall, disconnectedly and incoherently, upon the mind.

The impulse, however, which is so much a part of the life of literature in our immediate time—the refusal in any way to transfigure or to reconstruct or to try to impose a new order on the human reality—was expressed precursively not only in the area of the novel. In poetry, too, there was a marginal tradition contemporaneous with the classic modern movement that wanted only to be, in Carlos Williams' phrase, an "approximate co-extension with the universe."[16] In the *témoignages* of René Char and Henri Michaux on the French scene, or in the *collages* of Charles Olson and Williams himself on the American scene, we discern expressions of that anti-Platonic current in our century's poetry which is distinguished by the poet's habit of apprehending the world as simply there

15. Bernard Blackstone, *Virginia Woolf: A Commentary* (London, Hogarth Press, 1949), p. 10.
16. William Carlos Williams, *Spring and All* (Dijon, Contact, 1923), p. 27.

and as in no way itself proposing any sort of transfiguration. For William Carlos Williams a kitchen spigot is simply a kitchen spigot, and a wheelbarrow touched by rain is nothing other than itself; nor does *poiesis* involve any metaphysic of transubstantiation—it is simply a technique of resignation to the sheer welter of existence. In this, Williams was at one with such writers as Jorge Guillén and St.-John Perse, for whom Wallace Stevens may be regarded as having spoken, when, in "An Ordinary Evening in New Haven," he said, "We seek/Nothing beyond reality."

Nor is traditionalist modernism in the theatre without its anticipations also of post-modern tendency. For to move from Büchner's *Woyzeck* to Strindberg's *A Dream Play* and from Jarry's *Ubu Roi* to Pirandello's *Six Characters in Search of an Author* is to scan early and significant instances of the dramatic imagination finding in the imbalances and unresolved tensions of an open kind of form a way of circumventing any rigorous effort at giving a shape to the immense panorama of modern reality.

It is chiefly in the years since, roughly, World War II that the avant-garde in recent literature has taken an emphatically post-modern form. Here, as so often in the past, the French have played a decisive role, and it is the brilliant virtuoso, Alain Robbe-Grillet, who presents the crucial case. The novels which he has been producing since the early 1950s comprise the most widely publicized and perhaps the most important exhibit of that *nouveau roman* whose practitioners (Claude Simon, Michel Butor, Marguerite Duras, Nathalie Sarraute) represent today one major phase of the post-modernist insurgency. In addition to his considerable novelistic gifts, M. Robbe-Grillet has a genius for programmatic statement, and thus the essays which make up his little book *Pour un Nouveau Roman* (1963) constitute a notable landmark of the present time.

Robbe-Grillet's basic rejection—on which his whole theory of literature is based—is a rejection of what he considers to be the inordinate anthropomorphism of the inherited literary tradition. The tradition of Homer, Dante, Shakespeare, Tolstoi, and Proust is, for all its variousness, a tradition which, in his estimate of things, is deeply rooted in the old "cult of the 'human,' " and its method or system is an affair of analogy. It speaks, for example, of the weather as "capricious" or of the mountain as "majestic" or of the sun as "pitiless," as though the furniture of the world were drenched in human sentiments and moral values; and this analogical attribution of fancy *profondeurs* to the data of physical reality, this throwing of bridges across the gulf between man and the world, has the effect of suggesting, say, that "Mont Blanc has been waiting for me in the heart of the Alps since the tertiary era, and with it all my notions of greatness and purity!"[17] But if there is no "metaphysical pact" between man and the world—and Robbe-Grillet takes it for granted that there is none—then, he contends, it is simply fraudulent for the literary artist to render reality as if it were all an affair of "signification."

Not only must all analogical procedures be, therefore, discarded, but so too must the writer forswear essentialism of every kind, taking objective, phenomenological description as his legitimate and appropriate task; for, as he says, that dubious "interiority which Roland Barthes has called 'the romantic heart of things' " is in truth a "pseudo-mystery."[18] Nor is man himself in fact omnipotent; the world is not his "private property, hereditary and convertible into cash";[19] indeed, what is most remarkable about the world is simply that it *is*. "Around us, defying the noisy pack of our animistic or protective adjectives, things *are there*. Their surfaces are distinct and smooth, *intact*, neither suspiciously brilliant nor transparent."[20] What lucidity requires is that we achieve the ability to see, "through entirely unprejudiced eyes," without camou-

17. Alain Robbe-Grillet, *For a New Novel*, p. 56.
18. Ibid., p. 21.
19. Ibid., p. 29.
20. Ibid., p. 19.

flaging everything with "a continuous fringe of culture."[21] "Man looks at the world, and the world does not look back at him";[22] for, contrary to the traditional humanist illusion, the world itself is not bathed in signification; it is outside man, irredeemably other, and a truly mature literature is one which undertakes "to measure the distances—without futile regret, without hatred, without despair."[23]

M. Robbe-Grillet wants to propose—and most especially for the novel, which is his chief concern—that literary art in our time be submitted to a very drastic surgery. His declaration is that, given its general stagnation, it needs to be radically purged of all the old eloquence, the old myths of depth, the old anecdotalism, if it is to become anything more than "mere literature," if it is to become (in Giraudoux's phrase) "an evening school for adults." Total objectivity, "total impersonality of observation," may not, as he admits, be easily achievable. "But *freedom* of observation should be possible"[24] —such a freedom, that is, from conceptual encumbrances as will permit us lucidly to behold the world in its brute factuality and in its unyielding resistance to our conventional habits of ordering and apprehension. "Since it is chiefly in its presence that the world's reality resides, our task is now to create a literature which takes that presence into account."[25]

The creation of such a literature will entail not only a strict attentiveness to the fact that the objects of the world are *"there* before being *something,"* not only a refusal of the old anthropomorphism, but also full recognition of the fact that what is primarily true about the human presence itself is simply its thereness. Not only must the world itself not be rendered as if it were merely a vague reflection of the human spirit, but the "one serious, obvious quality" of man himself must be shown to be simply his presence, his thereness. The tradi-

21. Ibid., p. 18.
22. Ibid., p. 58.
23. Ibid., p. 74.
24. Ibid., p. 18.
25. Ibid., p. 23.

tional hero is very largely a creature of the author's commentary and interpretation, of what M. Robbe-Grillet calls "psychological analysis." But *le roman objectif* will forswear the old "sacrosanct psychological analysis," the old anthropocentrism; and it will exclude from itself what has traditionally been denominated as character for the sake of inviting the reader to reflect that human personality is not indeed "the means and the end of all exploration," that the person is not in fact omnipotent, and that the old cult of the human is, therefore, an obsolete irrelevance. And just as rigorously will *le roman objectif* expunge from itself what a traditional poetic of fiction calls story. For to tell a story which has a beginning and a middle and an end is to impose such an order upon the world as has the effect of domesticating it within an atmosphere of human value and sentiment; and not only is the old anthropomorphic fallacy thus reinstated, but the whole machinery of reversals and recognitions, of climaxes and denouements, also has the effect of implying what is in fact a lie —that events do but mask the "hidden soul of things" and that there are depths in experience which call for some sort of metaphysical transcendence. Thus Robbe-Grillet's prescription for what he takes to be the present malaise of fiction requires the extrusion of both characters and stories, and his intention, says the French critic Bernard Dort, is "to stick to zero."[26] He would have the novelist convert the world and the reality of man into a kind of frozen still life about which nothing at all really is to be said, about which no judgment is to be made, which is simply to be looked at, with entirely unprejudiced eyes.

M. Robbe-Grillet is not the sole theorist in the *nouveau roman* circle in France today: Michel Butor has produced two volumes of critical essays, and Nathalie Sarraute, whose own fiction is not always easily associable with the group, has given many of the circle's aims impressive formulation in her book *L'Ere du Soupçon*. But it is the pungent insolence and

26. Bernard Dort, "Are These Novels 'Innocent'?" *Yale French Studies*, no. 24 (Summer 1959), p. 24.

brilliant intensity of Robbe-Grillet's rhetoric which have given his manifestos a quasi-official status. However much the essays in *Pour un Nouveau Roman* were originally written, as he himself admits, in justification of his own novelistic practice, they do, nevertheless, present a remarkably useful summary of the general ethos made up by the fiction of such writers as Butor, Beckett, Mme. Sarraute, Jean Cayrol, Claude Simon, and numerous others—though, of course, since Robbe-Grillet is in no formal sense a legislator for the group, his theoretical work provides no exact chart of a movement representing a good deal of lively variousness and diversity.

Robbe-Grillet's novel of 1959, *Dans le Labyrinthe*, is an extreme example of this literature—a book which wants its reader, as the Preface tells us, "to see in it only the things, gestures, words, and events that he is informed about." An unnamed soldier, exhausted and ill, is lost in a strange city through whose snow-blanketed streets he wanders at night, having forgotten the name of the particular street for which he is looking. He carries a cardboard box which contains the last remaining possessions (a watch, a sheaf of letters, a ring, a bayonet) of one of his comrades who was killed at the front; and, since their forces have been defeated, he wants to deliver this package to a relative of the dead soldier before the enemy's occupation troops arrive in the town. But he has forgotten not only the street and the address for which he is headed but also the name of the person to whom his parcel is to be given and the appointed hour of their meeting. So his search goes on in a labyrinth, the progress of it moving through street after street after street of the snow-covered city. At a certain point he is led to an inn by a small boy, and, at another point, he is taken in and given refreshment by a young woman. A restless night is spent in a sort of hostel for disabled soldiers. Finally, he is fatally wounded by a reconnoitering patrol of the enemy forces. He dies, however, not on the streets but in the apartment of the young woman—who takes him in a second time—and to her he gives his package the contents of which are sorted out by a physician who says that he was too late to help the dying man. It is the physician's use of the possessive adjective of the first person ("my") to speak of his visit to the young woman's apartment which enables us to identify him with the "I" who, at the beginning of the novel, speaks in a closed room—on one wall of which there is an engraving that pictures a café scene containing the very characters (the soldier, the little boy, etc.) whom we are to meet in the course of the novel.

Despite the book's appearing to have been written from the standpoint of an impersonal omniscience, it seems, then, that the narrative point of view is really that of the physician, and the exploration of this puzzle yields some interesting and valuable insights into Robbe-Grillet's basic intention. All that I want at this point to remark, however, is the dominant and overriding impression with which the novel leaves us—which, as we remember the lost soldier's uncertain progress through the strange, dark city, is an impression of the maze-like geometry of deserted streets bisecting and intersecting one another, one intersection leading into another, this avenue being broken by that, one road being cancelled out by another, the whole labyrinth being eerily illuminated by street lamps which dimly reveal façades that seem all to be identical. Nothing seems to be explained, nothing seems to be connected with anything else. The whole is simply a "multiplicity of still-shots,"[27] like the script which Robbe-Grillet prepared for Alain Resnais' film, *L'Année dernière à Marienbad*. And the stillness in his novels, as in those of Beckett and Butor, makes one feel that Claude Mauriac is right in suggesting that a certain silence has descended upon much of the new *alittérature*;[28] it is, indeed, in Roland Barthes' phrase, a *degré zéro de l'écriture*.[29]

Thus we are now at a very considerable distance from the

27. Ben F. Stoltzfus, *Alain Robbe-Grillet and the New French Novel* (Carbondale, Southern Illinois University Press, 1964), p. 93.

28. See Claude Mauriac, *L'Alittérature contemporaine* (Paris, Albin Michel, 1958).

29. See Roland Barthes, *Le Degré Zéro de l'ecriture* (Paris, Editions du Seuil, 1953).

modern movement, which was a great effort—in the novel, in poetry, occasionally in the theatre—to give order and form to what was felt to be the essential formlessness of modern reality. Indeed, in the careers of men like Joyce, Mann, Eliot, and Rilke it was an effort so grand in its scope and so moving in its intensity as to have provided a generation with its chief model of the very idea of the imagination. For, in attempting to say what we mean by the term imagination, when we hark back to the language of Coleridge's *Biographia* and speak of what he called "esemplastic power," the power of giving form to the immense multifariousness of the world, it is, I suspect, these great heroes of the modern movement that we have most immediately in mind. And if the making of order be considered to involve a process whereby the mind gives its consent to some ruling myth which itself in turn confers intelligibility and coherence upon the whole of experience, then the central passion that lay behind classic modernism may be said to have been a great mythicizing passion.

But what we now face—say, in the work of so representative an artist as Alain Robbe-Grillet—is a violently mythoclastic literature which is guided by a conscience that tells the writer that he best "serves a burdened and perplexed creature" by refusing in any way at all to compete with the immense panorama of reality in our own late time. As it is made by many of those who express today the central impulse of the post-modernist insurgency, this is a refusal, it might be said, which situates the contemporary writer somewhere between Antioch and Alexandria.

The conjunction of the names of these two great cities of the Roman Empire does, of course, immediately put us in mind of the great controversy that raged in the early centuries of Christian history between the two principal schools of exegetical theory. Alexandria, in northern Egypt, from a very early time was deeply affected, in its theological tradition, by the distinguished Jewish Hellenist, Philo, whose eclectic tendencies had led him to hellenize Scripture and to find much of Greek philosophy in the Old Testament. By the third century, under the influence of Philo's allegorism and as a result of its further development by such Christian exegetes as Clement and Origen, Alexandria had become the major center in the ancient Church of the employment of allegorical methods of scriptural exegesis. The Alexandrians were, on the whole, an urbane group of thinkers who tended to be warmly responsive to Greek intellectual tradition, most especially to the Platonic sense of the preeminence of the spiritual world. And, given their eagerness to find "spiritual" meanings in the Old and New Testaments, the allegorical method commended itself to them as the most fruitful way of explicating the Bible's mysterious language of parable and metaphor.

The Antiochenes, on the other hand, were convinced that the allegorism of the Alexandrians was calculated to do nothing other than evacuate the biblical tradition of its solid historical reality. The basic theological tendency of the Church of Antioch, in other words, was Aristotelian rather than Platonist and historical rather than speculative and mystical. Thus its principal exegetes—men like Diodorus of Tarsus and Theodore of Mopsuestia and John Chrysostom—instead of looking for arcane spiritual meanings in scriptural texts, wanted rather to emphasize the historical reality of the biblical revelation and to ground all exegesis firmly in the letter of Holy Writ. Their historicism led them to offer a vigorous resistance to what they took to be the Gnosticizing tendencies of the Alexandrians. And, following the Council of Nicaea, the sharp divergences between the two schools became something enormously explosive in the great christological controversies of the fourth century, in which the Alexandrians very radically stressed the eternal and divine element of the Incarnation and the Antiochenes, with equal radicalism, stressed the human and historical side.

Now, if this bit of history be itself allegorized, in Alexandrian fashion, then these two cities of the ancient Middle East, Antioch and Alexandria, may be thought of as standing for two countries of the mind, two perennially opposed perspectives on the relative weight which is to be accorded the claims of history as against those of the imagination. If one's allegiance is to Antioch, one turns then to the concrete materialities of the objective world as the locus of the real, and it is assumed that all imaginative construction must be corrigible by norms which are firmly grounded in the things of actual history. But, if one's allegiance is to Alexandria, then one regards the human spirit as having its proper residence in what Henri Focillon calls *la vie des formes*, and man's highest capacity is held to be the "esemplastic power," the power of giving order and form to the contingency of historical existence. In Antioch the prevailing attitude is one of profound respect for the rough and ragged contingencies of the world, since here, it is believed, in the unhewn givens of concrete experience, we encounter the reality that Henry James defined as "the things we cannot possibly not know." But, in Alexandria the prevailing interest is in designing (in I. A. Richards' phrase) "speculative instruments" whereby a shape and a significance may be given to the immense panorama that lies before us. And the distance between the two cities is immense indeed.

But the interesting thing about the protagonists of the new modernism in our literary life today is that they are to be located in neither Antioch nor Alexandria. They are, to be sure, not inclined to enter into any sort of competition with reality, and the refusal of a writer like Alain Robbe-Grillet to replace Reality with Myth or to attempt any sort of transfiguration of the historical concrete would seem to indicate a firm rejection of Alexandria. But, then, such books as *Le Voyeur* and *Dans le Labyrinthe* do not, on the other hand, give us a sense of saturation in historical actuality: each is a skillfully contrived arabesque that has its limited fascination, but, amid the complicated geometry of M. Robbe-Grillet's *chosisme*, we descry too much of the stuff of our experience being left out to be able to regard these books as doing any kind of adequate justice to the human life-world. So determined, in short, is the artist not to compete with reality that reality ends up being very much left behind, and thus the writer's position appears, finally, to be equidistant between both Antioch and Alexandria—neither for Reality nor for Myth.

This middle region, between the two cities, is being colonized today not solely by the *nouveau roman* circle of Alain Robbe-Grillet in France. Many of these writers, to be sure, have determinedly staked out this territory. But they have neighbors, the most immediate no doubt being those artists who work chiefly not in the area of the novel but in the theatre and whose stage Martin Esslin has taught us to speak of as the Theatre of the Absurd.[30] Mr. Esslin's umbrella reaches over a number of Englishmen (Harold Pinter, Norman Simpson) and Americans (Edward Albee, Jack Gelber, Arthur Kopit); but the chief figures, again, are those who write in the French language (a group so diverse, however, as to include the Irishman Beckett, the Rumanian Ionesco, the Spaniard Arrabal, and the Russian Adamov).

Here, too, such properties of traditional literary fiction as character and story are very often relegated to the discard, for this is a dramatic imagination which, since it finds existence inexplicable and unjustifiable, is unwilling to use a theatrical machinery that might have the effect of suggesting that the world is in fact amenable to the ordering of dramatic *mythos*. Indeed, the theatre of playwrights like Beckett, Adamov, and Ionesco is, as Mr. Esslin says, very largely an affair of " 'pure theatre' and abstract stagecraft"—an affair, that is, simply of "exits and entrances, light and shadow, contrasts in costume, voice, gait and behavior, pratfalls and embraces, all the manifold mechanical interactions of human puppets in groupings that suggest tension, conflict, or the relaxation of tensions."[31] No discursively formulable generalization about anything is advanced. People are not shown moving into and through the

---

30. See Martin Esslin, *The Theatre of the Absurd* (Garden City, Doubleday [Anchor Books], 1961).

31. Martin Esslin, "The Theatre of the Absurd," *Theatre in the Twentieth Century*, ed. Robert W. Corrigen (New York, Grove Press, 1965), p. 230.

rhythms of fate and destiny, and what they do is not done out of rationally analyzable considerations of motive and intent. This stage does not even admit onto itself those passional conflicts arising out of the opposed purposes of men. What it presents instead is a radically situational tableau of happenings, but of happenings strung together on a temporal continuum which is simply an unending transition between "one damn thing after another," so that, if you ask what will happen next, the answer, as Mr. Esslin reminds us, is likely to be that anything may come next, since we are moving through an imaginative universe in which conventional probabilities have been suspended. Thus—in such a play as Beckett's *Godot*, for example—we do not get the gradual revelation of a basic principle or the gradual completion of a unifying pattern; but, rather, we are given a series of spectacles, a series of happenings and of concrete images, and it is their very concreteness which the dramatist, it seems, is principally concerned to render.

Mr. Esslin has perhaps too great a penchant for the usual counters of fashionable journalism, when it is dealing with one or another variety of existentialist radicalism. One regrets this, for the whole apparatus of the Absurd and the Human Condition entails a semantic which tends to suggest that in a play like Beckett's *Godot*, Ionesco's *The Bald Soprano*, or Adamov's *Ping-Pong* we are really encountering a *pièce à thèse* all over again; and thus it may be that the real intent of these dramatists is to some extent betrayed. For they, too, one feels, are often inclined to make a testimony something like Alain Robbe-Grillet's, that "the world is neither significant nor absurd,"[32] that it simply is. But, though Alexandria is thus bypassed, Antioch itself is not visible, either, on this horizon. In so representative a case as *Waiting for Godot*, despite the play's abundant allusiveness to the Passion story of the New Testament, one cannot but be impressed by how untouched it is by the kind of vibrant historicity that Erich Auerbach found

32. Robbe-Grillet, p. 19.

to be so notably characteristic of the biblical narrative.[33] Again, the artist's position seems to be at a point between Antioch and Alexandria.

Nor should it be supposed that this is, in any singular way, the position in our time of the Continental avant-garde. My chief examples, to be sure, have been European, but the general tendency I have been wanting to remark is not a singularly European phenomenon. I cannot, of course, in brief compass undertake any full conspectus of the present scene in literature. But, having now spoken of the *nouveau roman* movement and the Theatre of the Absurd, both of which are largely European developments, I should perhaps also mention, even if hastily, a somewhat parallel movement in the United States, chiefly by way of suggesting how pervasive is the basic impulse which appears to define post-modernist enterprise in contemporary writing.

What is here in view is a particular development in the American novel of, roughly, the last decade, and it is one which splays out in so many diverse directions as to make very difficult a quick notation. Nor has it been given that sharpness of programmatic definition that the *nouveau roman* movement and absurdist theatre have received in the numerous manifestos which their various advocates have issued. Nevertheless, in the work of such writers as Thomas Pynchon and John Barth, James Purdy and Richard Stern, Donald Barthelme, Bruce Friedman and Joseph Heller—and John Hawkes ought perhaps also to be included here—we can discern a particular current of sensibility, a kind of highly stylized vision, which establishes these novelists as constituting a distinctive force on the present scene, however reluctantly they may themselves regard one another as expressing a common tendency.

This movement has not yet received any widely recognized

33. See Erich Auerbach, *Mimesis: The Representation of Reality in Western Literature* (Princeton, Princeton University Press, 1953), chaps. 1–3.

name. Its designation has sometimes been made in the terminology of absurdism, but such a nomenclature tends to associate these writers too closely perhaps with their European contemporaries. They are sometimes referred to as specialists in "black humor"—a term whose clarifying power may be more apparent than real. Yet the tag "black humor" does at least have the effect of calling attention to what is one of the primary qualities of this literature—namely, a sort of dandyism of ironic preposterousness and larky, outrageous joking. As a term of specification, it may also emphasize the tendency of such writers as Barth, Pynchon, and Heller to create a fiction in which tragic and comic modalities jostle each other with enormous briskness and animation.

The predilection of these novelists for the commingling of tragic and comic forms does, of course, express a deep inclination toward the abolition altogether of formalizing structures. In an interview published shortly after the appearance of *The Adventures of Augie March* in 1953, Saul Bellow said: "I kicked over the traces, wrote catch-as-catch-can, picaresque. I took my chance."[34] It is a similar sort of chance that the Barth of *The Floating Opera* or the Heller of *Catch-22* appears to have taken. They are novelists who do not want greatly to fidget over "the art of the novel," for, given their sense of how largely the world itself is indeterminate and astonishing and intractable, their feeling seems to be that one had better write catch-as-catch-can, not bothering overmuch about controlling forms but trusting to the luck of the improviser, throwing the farcical together with the horrific, the arcadian with the gothic, the bitter with the sweet, and allowing one's fictions garrulously to sprawl out into the untidy formlessness of primary existence. In Thomas Pynchon's *V.*, in J. P. Donleavy's *The Ginger Man*, in John Barth's *The Sot-Weed Factor*, in Thomas Berger's *Reinhart in Love*, in Joseph Heller's *Catch-22*, we face, in short (in Leonard Meyer's phrase), an

34. Harvey Breit, "Talk with Saul Bellow," *New York Times Book Review*, September 20, 1953.

"antiteleological art,"[35] an art which, taking it for granted that the world is without discoverable purposes or goals, devotes itself therefore to random procedures, to the methods of improvisation, giving up any highly "structured syntax of pattern and form,"[36] in order that it may be truly open to the turbulent incoherence of reality.

As one contemplates many of the characteristic styles of the post-modern movement in literature of the present time —and I have barely even begun to catalogue the relevant evidence that might be marshaled—it does indeed appear that Saul Bellow's *Augie March* is expressing the new sensibility of the age, when, towards the end of his tumultuous adventures, he says: "To tell the truth, I'm good and tired of all these big personalities, destiny moulders, and heavy-water brains, . . . big-wheels and imposers-upon, absolutists." It is something very much like this that seems to be felt today by many of the most interesting writers on both the European and the American scene. They look back upon the classic modern movement of the great early decades of the century, and they face the various massive structures of meaning which that movement attempted to impose upon what Eliot called "the immense panorama of . . . anarchy which is contemporary history"; and, recalling this whole adventure, their feeling seems to be that, for all of the courageousness of spirit and brilliance of mind that distinguished the innovating pioneers of forty or fifty years ago, these big personalities, these destiny moulders, these imposers-upon, do not any longer embody an authentically contemporary style. For these were writers—a Yeats, a Mann, a Pound, an Eliot—who were proposing in a great way to compete with what one of Bellow's characters calls "the reality situation." But now, as it is felt, deep in our post-modern era—and at a point equidistant between Antioch and Alexandria—we cannot extricate ourselves

35. See Leonard Meyer, "The End of the Renaissance?: Notes on the Radical Empiricism of the Avant-Garde," *The Hudson Review*, 16, no. 2 (Summer 1963), pp. 169–86.
36. Ibid., p. 175.

from that general condition which Nathalie Sarraute speaks of as "suspicion."

"We have now entered upon an age of suspicion," says Mme. Sarraute[37]—by which she means the scepticism felt by the contemporary reader when the writer undertakes to offer him something more than simple, direct reports on matters of fact; and she also means the disbelief that is felt by the writer himself in the integrity of his own medium, when he finds it being used to purvey something like Goethe's "the beautiful, the good, the true." It is, in other words, such a suspicion as requires that the literary enterprise be placed in the service of nothing more fancy or complicated than facts, little facts— "the first blade of grass . . . a crocus not yet open . . . a child's hand nestling in the hollow of my own"; for, says Mme. Sarraute, "believe me, that's all that counts." It is such a reverance for *l'actuelle*, for the radical hecceity of the concrete, which constitutes the prompting force behind the recent abdication from any large "competitive" effort. But, as we have seen, this ostensibly Antiochene position is itself often held in too radical a way to yield any genuinely profound reappropriation of the whole fabric of the experienced world, and thus the result has tended to be a condition of exile from the two great Cities of the imagination, both Antioch and Alexandria being left uncolonized.

It was inevitable, then, that the new literature should seem, as it often does, to be short-circuiting the kinds of theological concerns that traditionalist modernism so actively advanced. Thus a formal theology that, through its encounter with the literary imagination, had found itself quickened not only in its sense of the modern climate but in its own self-understanding as well is bound to feel somewhat frustrated now, as it confronts a literature that rarely seems any longer to give off "intimations of the sacred,"[38] not even in the negative and

37. Nathalie Sarraute, *The Age of Suspicion: Essays on the Novel*, trans. Maria Jelas (New York, George Braziller, 1963), p. 57.
38. R. W. B. Lewis, *Trials of the Word: Essays in American Literature and the Humanistic Tradition* (New Haven, Yale University Press, 1965), p. 110.

dialectical manner of a Rimbaud, a Kafka, or a Camus. To be sure, the classic modern tradition did not itself make any large use of "the finished frames of [theological] doctrine"[39] and was in fact a very radically secular tradition. Yet it was a tradition committed to a search for ways of giving a new shape and significance to that "immense panorama" of which Eliot spoke; it was a tradition committed to the search for a new vision of the whole, and was thus deeply focused on the ultimate issues of human perplexity. So, however radical may have been its abjurations and negations, in being prompted by an extreme metaphysical passion, they could be regarded as but an inverted expression of how persistently the human voyager remains always the *homo religiosus*. But, now, literature is so bent on decontaminating itself of the old *profondeurs* and has moved so deeply into an "anti-teleological" phase that a strange new silence seems to have descended upon it—and not, as some may feel, the rich, fecund silence that theology has occasionally known in its own history (in the great traditions of negative and mystical theology), but a silence dry and unpromising and absolute. And the formal, systematic theologian might well be expected, therefore, to conclude that the conscience of this literature is indeed something so purist, and so ruthless in its exactions, as to have wellnigh annulled any possibility of further commerce between the two departments of culture represented by religion and literary art. Such a termination of the issue would, however, I am persuaded, be shortsighted and would, in effect, regrettably scuttle a lesson of still undiminished importance in which, among the great writers of this century, Franz Kafka and T. S. Eliot are the preeminent guides.

In his brilliant and bilious little book on Kafka, the German critic, Günther Anders, has declared—more emphatically and more pungently than perhaps any of Kafka's other critics have ever done—that "The meaning of [his] entire work is governed

39. Ibid., p. 111.

by his awareness of the 'death of God.' "[40] He recalls that remarkable section of the *Aphorisms* which is devoted to "Reflections on Sin, Pain, Hope, and the True Way," and he finds Kafka reflected in those royal couriers whom he imagines in his 45th "Reflection" as hurrying through the world, and who, "as there are no kings left, shout to each other their meaningless and obsolete messages."[41] Such a quixotic role, says Anders, was precisely that which was enacted by Kafka himself. For the unexampled art of this tortured Czech genius forms the prayer of a man who was in fact a "shame-faced atheist." In his writings the very sense of religious meaning as irrevocably lost is itself converted into a religious experience: "the coins of his despair [are changed] into the currency of positive belief,"[42] and the sense of ultimate ambiguity is so rendered as to give it the tonality of some direct awareness of Transcendence. So his elected role, Anders maintains, was that of "messenger to a king who does not exist."[43]

Quite apart from the valuation which this archconservative places upon Kafka's vision, he does see, I think, with a startling clarity, what it is that makes this remarkable writer so infinitely fascinating in our time. Anders himself, of course, can find nothing but sophistical duplicity and decadence in the example that is presented by an artist who continued to write religiously, despite his having fallen under the spell of "the Muse of Agnosticism." But, though it may be lamented by some, it is, nevertheless, a primary fact of our age, that we are deeply moved only by those religious writers who make us feel that whatever they have won in the way of certitude or hope has been just barely snatched out of abysses of unbelief. Most of us are not certain any longer as to what is the real shape of our world, or as to how to take hold of and express the deep-

40. Günther Anders, *Franz Kafka*, trans. A. Steer and A. K. Thorlby (London, Bowes and Bowes, 1960), p. 82.
41. Franz Kafka, "Reflections on Sin, Pain, Hope, and the True Way," no. 45, in *The Great Wall of China: Stories and Reflections*, trans. Willa and Edwin Muir (New York, Schocken Books, 1946), p. 289.
42. Günther Anders, p. 83.
43. Ibid., p. 82.

est things that are in us; and that man, whether secular or religious, who supposes himself to be outside this quandary is living in a fool's paradise. W. H. Auden said many years ago, in an oft-quoted remark, that "our dominant religious experience [today] . . . is of our distance from God." And this is an experience well-nigh universally known by the men and women of our age, however they may stand in regard to the great received traditions of faith. Paul Tillich told us twenty years ago that now, at the end of the modern period, even the believer, indeed most especially the believer, will find himself mirrored in "the man who longs for God and cannot find Him," in "the man who wants to be acknowledged by God and cannot even believe that He is," and in "the man who is striving for a new and imperishable meaning of his life and cannot [yet] discover it."[44] Thus it is that, in the whole sweep of the biblical narrative, there is perhaps no figure among its minor personages who touches deeper chords in us than that father of the possessed child who, when Jesus told him that "all things are possible to him that believeth," is reported in St. Mark's Gospel (9:24) to have cried out, "Lord, I believe; help thou mine unbelief."

It was both out of and to such a profound spiritual ambivalence that Kafka was always speaking. The guiding intention of his art is beautifully summarized in the "Reflections," most especially in the 104th, where, in talking about the nature of faith, he says, in his typically gnomic and concise manner:

> You do not need to leave your room. Remain sitting at your table and listen. Do not even listen, simply wait. Do not even wait, be quite still and solitary. The world will freely offer itself to you to be unmasked, it has no choice, it will roll in ecstasy at your feet.[45]

"You do not need to leave your room," not because the immeasurable amplitude of Creation does not extend infinitely

44. Paul Tillich, *The Shaking of the Foundations* (New York, Charles Scribners' Sons, 1948), p. 139.
45. Franz Kafka, p. 307.

beyond one's private chambers, but rather because stillness itself, when intense and concentrated, becomes a profound kind of patience that enables a man to consent, as it were, to what is spoken of in the 66th "Reflection" as "the indestructible element in oneself." Then it is that all striving stops, all attempts to bring reality to heel, all attempts to make the world submit to one's own conceptions of proper design and right order. Indeed, when the self has been thus silenced, then "the world will freely offer itself," or so it may be hoped, in the way of that which comes as a gift of grace. Thus what is being proposed, always with the subtlest indirection, in *The Castle* and *The Trial* and all the most characteristic instances of Kafka's art is that the cultivation of such a patience may well be our primary human task.

It is the kind of patience—which Keats called "negative capability"—that is explored more profoundly in Eliot's *Quartets* than in any other text of twentieth-century poetry, and most especially in those great passages of "East Coker" where we are told to

be still, and wait without hope
For hope would be hope for the wrong thing; wait without love
For love would be love of the wrong thing; there is yet faith
But the faith and the love and the hope are all in the waiting.
Wait without thought, for you are not ready for thought:
So the darkness shall be the light, and the stillness the dancing.[46]

Indeed, recalling that late story of Kafka's called "A Hunger Artist" in which he bodies forth his whole idea of the artist in terms of this tale about a man dedicated to the art of fasting, we may say that such a waiting, that such a patience, as both he and Eliot were in quite different ways exploring is a kind of Hunger-Art. And Hunger-Art, we may say, is simply the art of abstention, the art of doing without that which human selfhood needs for its felicity and fulfillment—whereby preparation is patiently made for the time when "the world will freely offer itself."

46. T. S. Eliot, "East Coker," *Four Quartets* (New York, Harcourt, Brace, 1943), p. 15.

Which brings us back to the immediate scene of our literature today, for is it not the case that, in many of its most characteristic modes, it seems itself to be a form of Hunger-Art? It seems, it is true, very often to be at a point equidistant between Antioch and Alexandria, and thus, as I have said, it appears to be neither for Reality nor for the Myth (that is, the Idea, the System, the imposed meaning). May this not be, however, but a strange sort of abstention, a kind of *askésis*, that, whether it is consciously intended as such or not, stands to be a most stringent *preparatio*? If this be so, as I very much suspect it to be, then the new literature, far from having emptied itself of moral and religious profundity, may well be (to borrow a phrase from "East Coker") moving "Into another intensity"—for further explorations, for a deeper acceptance of "the burthen of the mystery."

The new avant-garde in our literary life is by no means alone today, however, in presenting us with important examples of Hunger-Art. It is one of the interesting hallmarks of the age that, outside the realms of poesy, it is the theologian who often seems to be incarnating most vividly the image of the Hunger-Artist. And it is partly for this reason that theology, more than any other formal intellectual discipline, may well afford the finest kind of purchase upon the literary imagination in our time. The other humanistic sciences enjoy, of course, small successes in reducing some limited area of experience to manageability, and thus they are often lulled too quickly into a state of being "at ease in Zion." But the essential nature of its endeavor prompts theology to aim for a radically synoptic kind of vision of man's place and prospect; and, from its high vantage point, it cannot easily escape a recognition of the quandaries by which men are beset in this distressed century when they undertake to determine, in any really fundamental way, the true beginning and end of the human adventure. So it begins itself to be a form of Hunger-Art, and, in the realm of systematic thought, it therefore makes a good perspective from which to appropriate those forms of Hunger-Art that are to be found in the imaginative literature of the present time.

The truest exemplars of this new style in the forums of contemporary theology are not, however, I think, to be found among that handful of new American theologians who are today agitatedly reiterating Nietzsche's outcry of 1882 (in *The Gay Science*), that "God is dead." The distinguished German thinker, Gerhard Ebeling, is no doubt accurately reading our present situation when he asserts that "a doctrine of God today . . . is abstract speculation if it does not have the phenomenon of modern atheism before it from the start."[47] But those of Dr. Ebeling's colleagues in recent German theology—and chiefly Heinrich Ott—who, like himself, have been deeply influenced by the late phase of Martin Heidegger reveal perhaps a more authentic contemporaneity than the young Americans (Thomas Altizer, William Hamilton, and their various fellow travelers) who are espousing what they call "radical theology." The German radicals do, to be sure, accept Heidegger's testimony about ours being a time of profound dislocation in the things of the spirit, a time of failure and privation in which God, having "withdrawn," is absent. But they also accept his further testimony that, therefore, in an age which is "the No-more of the gods that have fled and the Not-yet of the god that is coming,"[48] man needs to try to be a good "shepherd of being"—a course that will involve not any aggressive attempt at mastery of the metaphysical situation or at forcing reality to yield up its innermost secrets but that will involve, rather, a "step backwards"[49] into what Heidegger calls "meditative thinking."[50] By "meditative thinking" Heidegger means such a patient openness to the primal realities of human existence as will permit them simply to *be*, and thus, finally, to "unveil" themselves before the gaze of the mind. "Primal

47. Gerhard Ebeling, *Word and Faith*, trans. James W. Leitch (Philadelphia, Fortress Press, 1963), p. 342.
48. Martin Heidegger, *Existence and Being*, trans. Douglas Scott et al. (Chicago, Henry Regnery, 1949), p. 313.
49. Martin Heidegger, *Essays in Metaphysics: Identity and Difference*, trans. Kurt F. Leidecker (New York, Philosophical Library, 1960), p. 65.
50. Martin Heidegger, *Discourse on Thinking*, trans. John M. Anderson and E. Hans Freund (New York, Harper & Row, 1966), p. 46.

thinking" is a mode of waiting; it is a form of listening, silently and patiently—to the voiceless Mystery of Being which finds its voice in man himself. The primal thinker, if we may put it so, lets Being be, he consents to be addressed by it, he allows it to find its articulation in his own profoundest acts of prayer, its utterance in his tongue—his discipline, in short, is a type of Hunger-Art.

But those young American theologians who have recently won a certain publicity for the jig that they dance on the grave of God prove how lacking they are in genuine relevance to the religious situation of our period by their quickness to convert perplexity itself into dogma and by the haste with which, as a consequence, they foreclose redintegrative possibilities. That contemporary theology, however, which has spoken to us most movingly is, I believe, deeply touched, all of it, by the attitude of waiting, by the attitude of "meditative thinking," and touched by the modesty and tentativeness which are a part of such an attitude. The grand style—the style of Aquinas and Calvin and Schleiermacher—is not, to be sure, a part of those theologians who have taken the firmest grip on the mind of our generation. It is not the Tillich of the three-volume *Systematic* who moves us most deeply, but the Tillich of *The Protestant Era* and *The Courage To Be* and the sermons. It is not Karl Barth in his role as system builder who is felt to speak to us most relevantly, but rather the passionate poet of the human mystery who is speaking, say, in that great section of the *Church Dogmatics* (III/2) which is entitled "Man in His Time." Nor are men like the late Dietrich Bonhoeffer, Rudolf Bultmann, the late Friedrich Gogarten, and Gerhard Ebeling men whose special genius lies in system-building. They are instead men who make us feel that they share with Gabriel Marcel the conviction that "to bear witness is to contribute to the growth or coming of that for which one testifies."[51] They also make us feel that they would be prepared to agree with Rainer Maria Rilke, when he says,

51. Gabriel Marcel, *Homo Viator: Introduction to a Metaphysic of Hope*, trans. Emma Craufurd (Chicago, Henry Regnery, 1951), p. 213.

be patient towards all that is unsolved in your heart and try
to love *the questions themselves* like locked rooms. . . . Do
not now seek the answers, that cannot be given you because
you would not be able to live them. And the point is, to
live everything. *Live* the questions now. Perhaps you will
then gradually, without noticing it, live along some distant
day into the answer.[52]

Indeed, it is very much along such a route as this that the
most creative theology of our period seems to be moving. It
is, to be sure, a theology that often seems to be more at home
in the world of doubt than in the world of faith, and whatever
it wins in the way of certitude or hope appears to have been
just barely snatched out of abysses of unbelief. But this is
simply the way things go, in this late and difficult time. Theology is not so much seeking answers as it is seeking a way
of helping us to live along some distant day *into* the answer:
it is a form of Hunger-Art which looks toward a new age,
when the Truth "will freely offer itself."

It is in their convergence toward this single point that we
may discern, I believe, a very remarkable collaboration, as it
were, between the theological imagination and the literary
imagination of the present time. Both bear the marks of a post-
modern temper. Neither wants any longer to risk the grand
style (whether that of a Yeats or a Mann, or that of a Brunner
or a Barth). Neither wants any longer to compete with reality,
whether in the manner of traditionalist literary modernism or
in that of the metaphysical grammar of the *theologia perennis*.
Both seem to be guided by a conscience that tells the theologian and the artist that the burdened and perplexed people of
our age are best served by being invited to be patient and to
wait, at a point somewhere on the road between Antioch and
Alexandria, where perhaps the horizons of the two Cities,
being equally visible, may, together, provide the occasion for
that moment which Heidegger's lexicon speaks of by resorting

52. Rainer Maria Rilke, *Letters to a Young Poet*, trans. M.D. Herter
Norton (New York, W. W. Norton, 1934), pp. 33–34.

to the Greek term *a-letheia*, which means the "unconcealing" or the "unveiling"—of the Mystery of Being. And it may indeed well be that at this point, midway between the two Cities, where one tries, with a great intensity of spirit, to wait and to be patient—that it is just here that there is to be found the one point of purchase which, just now, we can grasp, with any real confidence and integrity.

Chapter Three THE LITERARY
IMAGINATION
IN A TIME OF DEARTH

The characteristic literature of the present time—which begins already to take us deeply into the post-modern phase of our culture—is, as I have suggested in the previous chapter, a literature that may well be conceived as deserving the appellation Hunger-Art. For it is a literature that specializes in the art of abstention, the art of getting on without the consolations either of Reality or the Myth. Inheriting all the exactions entailed in the legacy of Flaubert, James, Conrad, and Joyce; of Baudelaire, Laforgue, Eliot, and Pound; of Ibsen, Strindberg, Chekhov, and Brecht, the writer of our period feels his principal obligation to be that of confronting the total reality of the contemporary scene. But the breadth and variousness, the indeterminateness and the immense multiformity of that scene are profoundly intimidating, and have the effect of convincing the literary imagination of the futility of any serious attempt to compete with the "new reality." The generation of 1914 could still conceive it to be the writer's vocation to forge in the smithy of his soul the uncreated conscience of his race, to master and somehow to subdue—at least by the formalizing power of art itself—the rampant disorder of the modern world. But—as in the previous chapter I was attempting not so much to document as to suggest—increasingly it is the tendency of our novelists and playwrights and poets to feel that, late now in these post-modern days of our history, their only *donnée* (as one critic has remarked of Sartre) is that

59

The Literary Imagination

nothing is given, that there are no paradigms spacious enough to comprehend the human scene of our time, and that the work of art can therefore be little more than an illustration of the world's opaque mysteriousness and contingency. The kind of large reconstructive effort undertaken by a Proust, a Yeats, a Stevens, or a Joyce can no longer, it is supposed, prove itself on the pulse of what Susan Sontag calls "the new sensibility." "Everything," as Bishop Bulter said, "is what it is and not another thing": things are just as they are, and the world is simply what it is—this, or something like it, seems more and more to be a basic assumption of the literature following in the wake of traditionalist modernism. "Man looks at the world," says Alain Robbe-Grillet, "and the world does not look back at him." So the extravagant *profondeur* is simply irrelevant. And one mark of the artist's authenticity will, therefore, be found in his forswearing any attempt at radically clarifying or transfiguring the human reality. A central impulse guiding the literary imagination today appears, indeed, to be a violently mythoclastic rejection of all schemes and stratagems whereby coherence and order may be conferred upon the weltered givens of experience.

Yet, strangely, the artist's refusal to replace Reality with Myth results in no significant enlargement of the grasp upon Reality. The great new commitment, to be sure, is to the concrete, not to some higher reality to which it affords access, not to some metaphysical meaning which it veils, not even to the volatile tropisms of one's own sensibility through which it may be filtered. What is rather being attempted is a return to things in themselves, for, as Nathalie Sarraute says (on behalf of a generation), "that's all that counts." The great flaw in the world is felt to be the flattening banality that is introduced by all the habits of the old "anthropomorphism" to which we have for so long been inured by a tradition that has encouraged us to take for granted a "metaphysical pact" between ourselves and "things." But, this pact being now at a discount, what is sought is an immediate encounter with things in themselves, as they exist before they are rendered spiritless and insipid by our codes and norms, by our concepts and values. Yet such a return to the concrete must, of course, inevitably be hung up on the fact that the actual human situation is never as Descartes imagined it, with consciousness and existence pitted against each other in radical duality. The world with which we have our actual transactions is never appropriable as something pristinely naked of human valuation: there is no such thing as " 'un-thought' reality."[1] And this may be partly why the new mystique of *l'actuelle* yields so imperfect a sense of the full, living historicity of the human life-world. The allegiance to a sceptical empiricism and the fascination with the contingent and the concrete are of a sort, in other words, that leave not only the Myth but also Reality itself behind.

So ours is a period-style that thrusts us into an "open situation,"[2] into that middle region between (as expressed in the mythography of the previous chapter) Antioch and Alexandria, the two great cities that polarize the world of the imagination. The literature that most clearly bears upon itself the stamp of contemporaneity seems to be making a double refusal, of both Reality and the Myth; and thus its precincts are those from within which the horizon of neither Antioch nor Alexandria is visible. Which is to say that the imaginaton of our period, as it finds reflection in the arts of the word, is without a "world," in something like Heidegger's sense of the term. In the highly eccentric lexicon fashioned in his great book of 1927, *Being and Time*, the term *Dasein*—which means literally "to-be-there"—is the term which is reserved for the radically distinctive element in human existence. In Heideg-

---

1. René Etiemble and Yassu Gauclère, *Rimbaud* (Paris, NRF, 1936), p. 141.
2. Though I make my own use of it, the term "open situation" I derive from Dietrich von Oppen; see his essay, "Man in the Open Situation," *Journal for Theology and the Church*, 2 ("Translating Theology into the Modern Age"), ed. Robert W. Funk (New York, Harper & Row, 1965), pp. 130–58. (This journal is an abbreviated English-language edition of the *Zertschrift für Theologie und Kirche*, edited by Gerhard Ebeling).

ger's vision, man is the creature whose unique vocation it is to be so much preoccupied with what it means to be that he deserves, therefore, himself to be conceived as *Dasein*. The essence of *Dasein* lies in its immitigable concern for the nature of its own reality. And "world," in the Heideggerian lexicon, is a characteristic of *Dasein*. For Heidegger the concept of "world" does not designate simply the total aggregate of everything present in the universe. It stands rather for that entire complex of unitive images and analogies and principles through which the whole welter of existence becomes the integral field of reality in which man actually dwells. It is in this way that the idea of "world" is considered to be inextricably involved in the idea of *Dasein*. And, preempting now this bit of Heidegger's rhetoric for another expository purpose, it may be said perhaps that, when the imagination can no longer enter either Antioch or Alexandria, its condition begins to be that of being unenclosed by any sort of "world"; its situation is an "open situation," and it finds itself committed to a time of dearth.

It is, then, through such a time that Martin Heidegger is today our great philosophic guide; and over many years, in the isolateness of his little mountain village of Todtnauberg in West Germany's Black Forest, he has been brooding, in a profoundly exciting way, on the shape that human life assumes in an open situation and on the peculiar vocation of the poet to venture out onto this uncertain terrain. The situation of man, at the end of the modern age, is, in Heidegger's reading of it, something open, in the sense of its being located in a great intervenient space, in a great *Between*. As he says, in the clumsy stiltedness of manner so typical of his strange rhetoric, ours "is the time of the gods that have fled *and* of the god that is coming. It is the time of *need*, because it lies under a double lack and a double Not: the No-more of the gods that have fled and the Not-yet of the god that is coming."[3]

The proposal that ours is a time of privation and dearth, of

3. Martin Heidegger, "Hölderlin and the Essence of Poetry," in *Existence and Being* p. 313.

need, occurs, to be sure, towards the end of an essay on Hölderlin and reflects Heidegger's fascination with the special sort of eschatological sensibility controlling Hölderlin's poetry. But it also reflects, of course, his equal fascination with that other mad eschatologist in modern German tradition, born in the year following Hölderlin's death, who brusquely proclaimed the death of God (or at least of all the old names and conceptualizations of God) in a book of 1882 curiously entitled *Die Fröliche Wissenschaft (The Gay Science)*. Indeed, it is Friedrich Nietzsche who marks for Heidegger one of the great decisive turning points in the history of what he speaks of as "the humanization of truth."[4]

The humanization of truth—the doctrine that truth resides in some human perspective rather than in Being itself—is, for Heidegger, the great disaster involved in Western intellectual history, because it entails a sundering of the primordial bond between the human spirit and what (by adapting a phrase of Teilhard de Chardin) might be called the *milieu ontologique.* To be sure, in *Being and Time* he had declared "world" to be an achievement of *Dasein,* and such an epistemology would itself seem to have entailed a perspectivist concept of truth. Within a few years after the appearance of this book, however, he appears to have concluded that its account of the relation between *Dasein* and Being was applicable only in a very rough sort of way to the more perfunctory transactions of everyday that man has with reality; whereas, in the great decisive and extreme situations of human existence, it is not in man but in Being itself that truth is found to be resident. So, in a series of works belonging to the 1940s,[5] he began to

4. The view of Nietzsche is set forth in his *Nietzsche 1, 2* (Pfullingen, Günther Neske, 1961).

5. The principal documents in the case are perhaps *Platons Lehre von der Wahrheit* (Bern, Francke, 1942); *Vom Wesen der Wahrheit* (Frankfurt am Main, Klostermann, 1943); and *Über den Humanismus* (Frankfurt am Main, Klostermann, 1949). To these may be added the later works in which the critique of Kant is set forth—*Der Satz vom Grund* (Pfullingen, Günther Neske, 1957); *Die Frage nach dem Ding* (Tübingen, Max Niemeyer, 1962); and *Kants These über das Sein* (Frankfurt am Main, Klostermann, 1963).

launch a fierce polemic against the whole heresy of "humanism," wanting now most emphatically to insist upon the non-humanistic orientation of his own thought.

Heidegger's basic conviction now is that all encounters between the Self and the Not-self—the terms are not his—occur, inevitably, within the environing milieu of Being, and that all the referential thrusts of human intelligence outward beyond itself are confirmable only in consequence of this encompassing *Plenum* whose "unhiddenness" does indeed make it possible for the Self to meet the Not-self in an act of cognition. The locus of truth, in other words, is not in this or that perspective (or category, or proposition, or system) that may be imposed upon reality, but is rather in the "unhiddenness" or transparency of Being; which is to say that truth is not an achievement but a gift, something granted and received.

But, as Heidegger argues, the assumption perennially informing the Western tradition has been that truth is resident in the schemata of human intelligence. The project of "humanizing" truth was first launched by the Greeks, preeminently by Plato, whose theory of Ideas did in effect, he maintains, attribute ultimate reality to what were nothing more than projections of human reason. The traditional Platonist will no doubt be scandalized by Heidegger's insistence that the Platonic Idea is nothing more than a concept; but—conventional textbook scholarship to the contrary (and he needs no instruction in this mode)—this, nevertheless, is his claim, that it is simply an audacious postulate, reified into Eternity. Thus the great bequest of Platonism to Western mentality has been the superstition that truth follows upon a proper deployment by the intellect of its own counters and that, in the ascending scale of ontological priority, certain human principles and idealities hold the sovereign place.

Heidegger finds an essentially identical error in medieval Scholasticism, where (as in Aquinas) truth is understood to consist in the "adequation" of the intellect to things as they are. This same view of truth as an achievement of human intelligence he finds being carried into the early modern period by Descartes, whose *Cogito* only signalized again how persistently the philosophic tradition remains (as Alfred Whitehead long ago remarked, though from a standpoint rather different from Heidegger's) but "a series of footnotes to Plato."

In Heidegger's reading of the Western tradition, this anthropocentric account of the world as an essentially human "project" gained even more emphatic expression in the critical philosophy of Kant which, after denying the possibility of our knowing things in themselves, went on to locate the ground of all objectivity in the synthetic categories with which the self orders its experience, thus making man himself the final and absolute measure of all truth. And so it comes to be that, for Heidegger, it is but a step from Kant to Nietzsche—and to the end of the whole Western experiment in humanization. For he who in 1882 announced the death of God was in effect embracing, in a violently strident way, what the whole antecedent tradition had been moving toward—the impertinence of regarding the world as itself simply an image of man. Nietzsche's according an ultimate status in reality to "the will to power"—to the principle of human assertiveness—did, in other words, entail, essentially, nothing more than a radicalization of what since Plato had been perennially inherent in the tradition; for the whole drive of the *philosophia perennis* is towards the assertion that man dwells, uncompanioned and alone, in a universe that is very largely of his own creation. Nor is this assessment of the meaning of our received tradition, for Heidegger, merely something which it is interesting for intellectual historians to contemplate. On his account, it is precisely in the humanization of reality in the West that we may find the explanation of the great malaise that blights the world now, at the end of the modern period—which is a disquiet arising out of the discovery that the triumphs of our scientific technology have been purchased by such an unbridling of "the will to power" as has sundered our most elemental bonds with nature and resulted in a wholly artificial environment for human life.

The Literary Imagination

At the heart of our culture there is, Heidegger suggests, a profound perversion, a great imbalance that needs correction. At the end now of (as he nominates it) the History of Being in the West, what is lost is simply Being itself, and the great task awaiting the imagination is the recovery of a range of sympathy and conscience that will permit us to deal with the world in terms other than those simply of aggressive action. Our traditional habits of preference for what is assertive and bold and aggressive do indeed account for much that is distinctively a part of the impressive achievement of Western culture, but what Heidegger calls *the will to will* may also, as he sees, have the effect of so committing us to an essentially manipulative approach to reality that all attentiveness to the sheer ontological weight and depth of the world is lost. And this is precisely the sort of loss that he believes to threaten in such an advanced technological culture as our own, where our great temptation is to be so bent upon bringing the world to heel that we risk its becoming totally devoured by the engines of our science and ideology. In such a time our great need is somehow to bring the usual traffic of our acting and thinking to a stop, in order that we may deepen ourselves down into the kind of profound repose and expectancy that will permit our becoming permeable again by the integral reality of the world. When we have reentered those "quiet mysterious depths,"[6] where "all the forces of the soul [are] . . . gathered together in quietude, . . . in a state of virtuality and dormant energy,"[7] then the whole world of Creation seems to be resounding in ourselves, and we begin to be overtaken by a happy impulse (in Jonathan Edwards' phrase) simply to "consent to Being." Then it is at last that the truly human posture vis-à-vis the world is achieved, and the name which Heidegger gives to it is that which forms the title of his little book of 1959—*Gelassenheit:* submission, abandonment, surrender, ac-

6. Thomas Carlyle, "Characteristics," *Essays* (Boston, Brown and Taggard, 1860), *3*, 9.
7. Jacques Maritain, *Creative Intuition in Art and Poetry*, Bollingen Series, xxxv, 1 (New York, Pantheon Books, 1953), p. 242.

quiescence. It is, he maintains, only when *the will to will* has been thus subdued and when we have deeply surrendered to the unplumbed Mystery of Being that the Mystery begins to be transparent before the gaze of the mind; it is only when we have consented to be *stupid* before the absolute presence of Being that it begins, translucently and radiantly, to disclose itself.

But, after the long experiment of our culture in "humanization," by what means is it to be expected that we may overcome our "forgetfulness" of Being? This is for Heidegger, one feels, the central question needing to be raised in our own late and problematic time, and it is just as the issue begins to be posed by the logic of his own thought that his answer begins already to be in view. For, untroubled by the sense of scandal that he may thereby give to his fellow philosophers, the remarkable position taken by this audacious thinker is that it is precisely the vocation of the poet to bring us once again into the region of fundamental reality.

The epigones like now to make arcane distinctions between the earlier Heidegger (of *Being and Time*) and "the later Heidegger," between the phenomenologist of *Dasein* and the metaphysician for whom the primary reality is no longer *Dasein* but Being. For this later Heidegger the principal fact about our culture concerns its dominance by technology. In his view of the modern situation, the sovereign passion controlling our period is one which prompts an effort at winning mastery of the world: it is a passion to control and to manipulate both nature and human life itself, and this technological orientation is something long prepared for by a culture whose philosophic strategists so "humanized" the predominant conception of reality that Being came to be regarded as that which is to be grasped and manipulated and controlled. The consequence is that we now find ourselves enveloped by that desiccating "second nature" comprised of the wholly artificial environment which technological enterprise throws round human life. In this extremity, any profound renewal of the human spirit will require that it unlearn its habit of approaching the world as something to be "attacked,"[8] in the manner of a scientific experiment or technological project. What must be learned again is the discipline of "letting-be"[9] What Is, of throttling *the will to will* and of *surrendering* to the radically immanent presence of Being. It is in just this discipline that the poet, as Heidegger maintains, offers a unique and an indispensable tutelage. His whole purpose is to stir and quicken within us an awareness of the irrevocability by which the things of this world are as they are. Much of Heidegger's writing of the last thirty years is integrally related to his theory of literature, even when, in a given work, his immediate theme may happen in no way to touch explicitly on the subject of poetry; but, for a reconstruction of this phase of his thought, the most crucial documents are two collections of essays, the *Interpretations of Hölderlin's Poetry (Erläuterungen zu Hölderlins Dichtung)*[10] and the book called *Paths in the Forest (Holzwege)*.[11] The language of these essays—like that of the entire œuvre to which they belong— is, in its obscurity and elusiveness, an achievement remarkable even in a tradition whose systematic thinkers have rarely been notable for their stylistic clarity. But, in so far as the true intention of this strange rhetoric is discernible at all, it would seem that, for Heidegger, it is most especially the distinctive office of the poet to make us look at the various concrete realities of experience with the kind of attentiveness that will permit their being disclosed "in the starkness and strangeness of their being what they are."[12] The artist seeks to bring us into a relationship of intense intimacy with a given event, with some quite specific phenomenon. What he invites is an attitude of enthrallment before the sheer specificity of whatever may be the object which is holding up for attention. The

8. See Martin Heidegger, *Discourse on Thinking*, p. 88.
9. See Martin Heidegger, "On the Essence of Truth," *Existence and Being*, pp. 319–51.
10. Frankfurt am Main, Klostermann, 1944.
11. Frankfurt am Main, Klostermann, 1950.
12. H. D. Lewis, "Revelation and Art," *Morals and Revelation* (London, Allen and Unwin, 1951), p. 212.

poetic world—that is, the world of literary art in general
—is rooted in the concrete particularity of lived experience.
Whereas the scientific view of the world is ultimately predatory, driving toward possession and mastery and control,
"poetic art, in its deepest aspect, is a way of loving the concrete, the particular, the individual"[13]—a way, as Heidegger
would say, of simply letting things be. The poet does not want,
as it were, to put things on their good behavior by making
them obedient to the well-driven machine of the Idea; rather,
he wants to reconstitute our perceptual habits in a way that
will restore to us the innocence which is simply enthralled by
the bright actuality of the things of earth.

The poet, then, in Heidegger's view, might be said to be an
adept in the art of "paying heed"—which is why he can say
in the *Holzwege* that, in a work of art, "truth is at work" (p.
45). Truth is at work, because the carefulness with which the
poet pays heed to the things of earth has the effect of bringing
them "into the Open." Which is to say, in Heidegger's terminology, that the poet is he who "hails" Being, since Being itself is nothing other than "the Open"—that immediate and
luminous presence constituting the inner cohesion whereby
things are enabled simply to be what they are.

In the essay on "The Origin of a Work of Art" in the *Holzwege*, for example, Heidegger speaks of a Van Gogh painting
of a pair of farm shoes, and he invites us to compare the artifact with the shoes themselves. The actual shoes are merely a
piece of what he calls "equipment," and the "equipmental
being" of the shoes consists, he says, in their "serviceability."
The old peasant woman who uses them, who trudges in them
day by day through the dampness of the soil and the furrows
of her fields, knows these shoes in their equipmental being,
and knows them without having to take thought. But we, as
we look at the shoes, do not begin to comprehend their essential nature—how they vibrate with "the silent call of the

13. Nathan A. Scott, Jr., *The Broken Center: Studies in the Theological Horizon of Modern Literature* (New Haven, Yale University Press,
1966), p. 179.

earth," how they slide along "the loneliness of the field-path as evening declines," how they are pervaded by "the wordless joy" of "ripening corn"—until Van Gogh's painting opens them up out of their captivity unto themselves and into what they most emphatically are in their radical actuality. It is the work of art that brings into the open that which has "withdrawn" behind the shoes but which, once it is fully revealed, is seen to be that which in truth imparts "presence" to the shoes—and this is nothing other than Being itself whose location is necessarily always in finite things behind which it withdraws. When these things are truly paid heed to, so that they are brought into the open, what is then in view is nothing less than Being itself, for that is what Being is: it is simply that effulgence wherewith the things of earth are enabled to have an emphatic and persisting presence.

So poetic art, because it renders us alert to the concrete realities of the world in the dimension of presence, brings us into the region of Being, since Being itself is nothing other than Presence. But, in performing this kind of function, poetry is for Heidegger simply the crucial instance of language in general, since, as he says in the *Holzwege*, the primary task of language is not merely to be a technique of signification but "to bring beings as such for the first time into the Open" (p. 61). Indeed, man does not have a "world," does not have any sort of unified matrix of meanings and relations in which to dwell, unless he has a language, a way of declaring what things "appear to be as they come into the Open" (*Holzwege*, p. 61). This, one imagines, is the insight that he takes to be implicit in the saying of Hölderlin for which he has such a great liking, that "poetically,/Man dwells upon the earth."[14] Man dwells upon the earth—in a really human way—only in so far as he transforms "earth" into "world," and he can have a world only if he has language, only if he has a way of being open to Being and of naming the things of earth in which Be-

14. See the essay on "Hölderlin and the Essence of Poetry" in *Erläuterungen zu Hölderlins Dichtung;* also in *Existence and Being*, pp. 293–315.

ing resides: which is to say that he can have a world only as he manages in some manner to be a "poet."

But, of course, though our human situation requires us to dwell poetically on the earth, in the ordinary, day-to-day transactions of life, we become creatures of routinized modes of thought and feeling that permit only just so much attentiveness to reality as is requisite for the immediate fulfillment of our practical purposes. We hasten to and fro in the world, from day to day, from one occasion to another, hearing only so much of this and seeing only so much of that as the urgencies of our common affairs allow. "Just as meat to the dog is something to be eaten, and the cat simply something to be chased, so the chair to a tired man or an executive is simply something to be sat on; and to the thirsty man water, however lovely its flow or sparkle, simply something to be drunk."[15] So it is, ordinarily, throughout the whole gamut of our living: the environing world in which we are set is rarely perceived as anything primitively arresting or marvelous: things are merely cues for action or signals of desire—the bare minimum of all that would be there, were we to take the trouble of paying heed. Thus our "experience is full of dead spots,"[16] everything, as it were, incidental and pragmatic, gross and philistine.

This impoverishment that is normally a part of ordinary experience is, however, in Heidegger's sense of things, very greatly deepened in a technological culture such as our own, where inorganic nature becomes merely an affair of pointer-readings and human biology itself becomes the experimental material of a casually deliberate medical science, and where a great screen is thrown up—by all our gadgets and artifacts—between man and the primitive realities of the earth. It is in such a climate that human life begins to descend into a most radical "godlessness."

Recurrently in his writings of the last thirty years, but most especially in the essays on Hölderlin, Heidegger has spoken in

15. Irwin Edman, *Arts and the Man* (New York, W. W. Norton, 1939), p. 16.
16. Ibid., p. 18.

a curiously veiled and gnomic way about "the gods." He says, for example, that we dwell in a period between that in which the gods "fled" and that in which they will return, and he seems to regard it as one of the chief signs of the authentic poet that he should have a very profound sense of this present time as a time betwixt and between. Indeed, he defines the poet as "one who has been cast out . . . into [this] . . . *Between,* between gods and men."[17] He speaks of the poet as one who consents to take his stand in the presence of the gods and who *names* the gods. Similarly cryptic references to gods appear in various other contexts. But, ambiguously as the term behaves in the logic of Heidegger's thought, its effect has been sufficiently tantalizing to lead some of his theological interpreters apparently to assume that it is merely a somewhat eccentric locution carrying, at bottom, a traditionally monotheistic meaning.[18] Yet so to construe the import of his testimony is, I believe, to misconstrue it; for, despite the short shrift he gives any sort of conventional atheism and despite the deeply religious tenor of his entire work, his basic intentions are not those of Christian apologetics, as he has himself been at pains to remind us on more than one occasion. So it is surely an illicit maneuver to singularize Heidegger's "gods" and then to interpret what he says about their "return" as simply his figurative way of anticipating the coming end of Nietzschean nihilism, when the God of traditional Christian experience will no longer be absent and will once again return in power and glory.

But if the term "gods" is not translatable as God, how, then, is it to be understood within the framework of Heidegger's thought? The issue is not to be easily resolved, for the

---

17. "Hölderlin and the Essence of Poetry," *Existence and Being,* p. 312.
18. See, for example, two essays of Stanley Hopper's—"On the Naming of the Gods in Hölderlin and Rilke," *Christianity and the Existentialists,* ed. Carl Michalson (New York, Charles Scribner's Sons, 1956), pp. 148–90; and his Introduction, *Interpretation: The Poetry of Meaning,* ed. by Stanley Romaine Hopper and David L. Miller (New York, Harcourt, Brace and World, 1967), pp. ix–xxii.

term does, of course, function figuratively and may not, therefore, be fully reducible at all to any definition of a univocal
sort. But I would hazard the proposal that the basic consisten-
cies of his vision are least violated when, by "gods," Heidegger is taken to mean whatever it is that holds the world together and "assembles" it into a stable unity. By "god" we
may assume, I think, that he means that ultimate *power* of Being which permits things to sojourn on the earth and which
guarantees to reality the character of permanence and stability
and trustworthiness.[19] And his affirming it to be a part of the
poet's office to *name* the gods is but his oblique manner of
reasserting the radically cognitive way in which the literary
experience thrusts outward, beyond itself, toward those realities that, in the most basic way, encompass the human enterprise.

So "godlessness" in Heidegger's lexicon is not properly
equated with something like Nietzsche's "death of God"; it
speaks, rather, of that profound inattentiveness to the essential fabric and texture of the things of earth which becomes
epidemic in a technological culture, where everything that
faces man is approached with an intention simply to control
and manipulate and where, as a consequence, nothing is seen
or experienced in the dimension of Holiness. The Holy (*das
Heilige*) makes its way into Heidegger's thought through his
meditation on that untitled poem of Hölderlin's which begins
"Wie wenn am Feiertage . . ."—"As when on a holiday . . ."[20]
He takes it to be a term required of Hölderlin himself by his
fidelity to the sheer presence of Being in the finite realities of
the earth. And this is precisely what Holiness means for Heidegger: it is that power and form wherewith a thing is what

19. In his book *Earth and Gods: An Introduction to the Philosophy
of Martin Heidegger* (The Hague, Martinus Nijhoff, 1961), Vincent Vy-
cinas' interpretation of Heidegger's notion of "gods" soars off on a
highly speculative flight (see chap. 5), and I remain unconvinced of its
cogency or even that much of it has any clear relevance at all to what is
actually being said in the Heideggerian texts. Nevertheless, my own
"demythologization" has been influenced to some extent by his exegesis.
20. See *Erläuterungen zu Hölderlins Dichtung*, pp. 47–74.

it is—whose penumbra of mystery naturally evokes an attitude of awe and astonishment.

Martin Buber reminds us that we may consider a tree as though it were merely a stiff column against a background of delicate blue and silver in a picture; or we can perceive it as an affair of vital movement, in its "ceaseless commerce with earth and air"; or we may simply regard a given tree, in its formation and structure, as an instance of a species; or we may "subdue its actual presence and form so sternly" as to recognize it only as an expression of certain laws governing the ways in which "the component substances mingle and separate"; or, again, the particular tree may be so subsumed under a given type that it is thought of only as belonging to some scheme of numerical relations. But, then, as he also reminds us, we may be so seized by "the power of exclusiveness" in the given tree that we find "everything, picture and movement, species and type, law and number, indivisibly united"[21] in the one tree that confronts the eye. Heidegger would say, I think, that what, in this case, we are seized by is nothing other than the *presence* of *this* tree; it is simply that most primitive of all realities that we are claimed by—namely, the power of Being itself. And if we can manage not to regard the land on which the tree stands as merely a piece of real estate, to be cleared perhaps for a suburban housing development; if we can manage not to regard the tree as merely a piece of timber to be cut down and converted to some useful purpose; if we can manage so to subdue *the will to will* as to confront this tree in an attitude of "letting-be," so that we can really be laid hold of by the sheer presence of Being in the tree, then, Heidegger would say, we shall find that what indeed we are most essentially seized by is that which is Holy in the tree—for the Holy, he declares, is simply the "advent" (*Kommen*) of Being itself.

When man becomes so enwrapt in the spirit of modern

---

21. Martin Buber, *I and Thou*, trans. Ronald Gregor Smith (Edinburgh, T. & T. Clark, 1937), p. 7.

technological enterprise that he loses any capacity for reverential awe before the radical holiness of Creation, then human life begins to descend into the Profane. As the whole drift of the modern period reveals, it is possible for a culture to become so fixed in its lust for winning mastery of the things of earth that all appetite is lost for what Wordsworth in Book II of *The Prelude* calls "the sentiment of Being." That is to say, we can become so mesmerized by our own human purposes and so committed to an essentially manipulative and predatory attitude towards the world that we defraud ourselves of any capacity to marvel at the generosity with which things are steadied and supported by the power and presence of Being. To whatever extent, however, a man fails to be attentive to what Gerard Manley Hopkins called that "pitch of self" which distinguishes each bird, each tree, each flowing stream, each bit of Creation, then he is, of course, to that extent by way of losing any full sense of that pitch of self which distinguishes his own reality—as Hopkins put it, "that taste of myself, of *I* and *me* above and in all things, which is more distinctive than the taste of ale or alum, more distinctive than the smell of walnutleaf or camphor."[22] When there is no longer any sense of grandeur in the "shining from shook foil," or of splendor in "the ooze of oil/Crushed," when there is no longer any lively sense of "the dearest freshness deep down things,"[23] then a great descent has begun—into that deprived condition that Martin Heidegger would nominate as "godlessness."

In such a time—of dearth, of inanition, of godlessness—Heidegger believes that the vocation of the poet inevitably becomes something pastoral and priestly. It is most especially the mission of the poet to be a watchman (*Wächter*) or shepherd

22. *The Note-Books and Papers of Gerard Manley Hopkins*, ed. Humphry House (London and New York, Oxford University Press, 1937), p. 309.

23. Gerard Manley Hopkins, "God's Grandeur," *Poems of Gerard Manley Hopkins*, ed. Robert Bridges (London and New York, Oxford University Press, 1938), p. 26.

(*Hirt*) of Being, as it emerges in the things of earth.[24] And his meditations on the poems of Hölderlin that speak of the poet as a wanderer journeying homeward[25]—"*Heimkunft/An die Verwandten*" ("Homecoming/To the Kinsmen") and "*Andenken*" ("Remembrance")—lead him to conclude that, when "forgetfulness" of Being has become the primary apostasy, then the poet must undertake to initiate in us a process of "remembrance" and to lead us homeward, back into "proximity to the Source."[26]

In the logic of Heidegger's metaphor, the process whereby the imagination recovers "the sentiment of Being" entails a "journey" because Being is "distant" and far away (*fern*).[27] It is far away simply because it is never to be encountered nakedly and in itself, but only in and through the things of earth which it supports and whose presence it establishes; which is to say, in the language of traditional philosophy, that Being is a transcendental, a reality which the imagination moves toward only by moving through the contingent and finite realities of immediate experience. Though Being is in this way "withdrawn," it is yet, paradoxically, also "near," since its presence in the things of our immediate experience is precisely that which enables them to *be*, and thus to be *near*. Hence it is, as Heidegger sees it, that, in a time of dearth, the renewal of the life of the imagination can be conceived to involve a kind of journey. The journey is back to the "Source" (*Ursprung*), since that is what Being is; and to return into proximity to the Source is to be once again "at home," since Being is nothing other than the original and proper domain of

---

24. Though Heidegger's famous metaphor about the "shepherding" of Being is adumbrated at many points in his writings, its central locus is in the *Über den Humanismus* (*Letter on Humanism*, pp. 75, 90)—where he says, "Man is the shepherd of Being" ("*Der Mensch ist der Hirt des Seins.*"). Though *man* is here said to bear this office, the *Letter on Humanism* implies that it is a vocation whose ideal exemplifications are to be seen most clearly in two special types of man—in "the thinker" (*der Denker*) and "the poet" (*der Dichter*).
25. *Erläuterungen zu Hölderlins Dichtung*, pp. 9–30, and pp. 75–143.
26. Ibid., p. 23.
27. Ibid., p. 138.

76

the human spirit. And since to be brought back into the neighborhood of Being is to have been put in mind again of that which had been forgotten, the journey homewards is also conceived to be a process of remembrance or recollection.

In the contemporary world of Anglo-American poetics, given its empiricist sobriety and its impatience with any sort of Longinian aesthetic of elevation and transport, the whole tenor of Heidegger's reflections may seem excessively inflated and hyperbolic. But always, I think, he does in fact have in view the concrete actuality of *poiesis*, and everything that he has to say about the poet's openness to the Holy, about his "naming the gods" and his bringing us homeward to the Source is but his way of asserting that the poet supervises language with such cogency and adroitness that we find ourselves being thrust onto new levels of heightened perception, where we no longer simply take for granted the common things of earth and where, performing again an act of genuine attention before the world that confronts us, we recover what is perhaps the most primitive of all sensations—the sense of astonishment that there is something rather than nothing, thus experiencing the "shock of Being."[28]

In his brilliant little book of thirty years ago, *Arts and the Man*, the late Irwin Edman recalls a story of Stephen Crane's about three shipwrecked men adrift in a small boat on an agitated sea. The opening sentence of the story, he reminds us, is, "They did not see the color of the sky." "So intent were they upon the possibilities of being saved that they had no time, interest, or impulse for seeing the color of the sky above them."[29] But what Heidegger wants to assert is that the whole job of the poet—in his office as priest—is so to intensify our awareness, our vision, of the concrete realities surrounding

28. The phrase derives from similar phrases of Paul Tillich's—"ontological shock" and "metaphysical shock"; see his *Systematic Theology, 1* (Chicago, University of Chicago Press, 1951), pp. 113, 163, 186. Tillich's concept of the "ontological shock" is, however, but one of many other usages in his work attesting to the probability of his having been far more profoundly influenced by Heidegger than he ever acknowledged or than his interpreters have thus far discerned.

29. Irwin Edman, p. 27.

us that, instead of moving constantly "among the abstract possibilities of action,"[30] human sensibility may be reinstated into a kind of pure alertness to (as I spoke of it earlier) the sheer ontological weight and depth of the world. "I require of you only to look," says St. Theresa—and it is, says Heidegger, by making us gaze, by making us look, at the things of earth that the artist disarms us of that penchant for manipulation and use characteristic of the predatory spirit in which we normally approach the world; he invites us instead to approach it in the spirit of *letting-be*, to offer a kind of *Amen* to the various finite realities that make up the earth, since, in so far as they are truly present to us, their presence is seen to be consequent upon their being rooted in the creative Ground of Being itself. Using a phrase that John Crowe Ransom once bestowed upon a collection of his essays, we might say that Heidegger's testimony—and in this he surely adumbrates, in his own quite special way, a perennial axiom—is simply that it is the function of literary art to enliven and deepen our cognizance of "the world's body,"[31] to the point of enabling it to become for us a "glass of vision."[32] This, as he maintains, is what it is uniquely within the power of the literary imagination to confer upon us in a time of dearth.

Then, there is a final emphasis which deserves to be thought of as also a part of Heidegger's theory of literature, though, in his own writings, it actually figures not so much as a part of his account of *poiesis* as it does as a part of his account of the drama of *thought*. What is here in view is the duality in Heidegger's thought between the two great roles that are enacted in the adventure of man's encounter with Being—the role of the poet (*der Dichter*) and the role of the thinker (*der Denker*). That is to say, the path into Being may be by way either of poetic art or of systematic thought. But Heidegger's whole style of reflection tends so much, in effect, to convert

30. Ibid., p. 29.
31. See John Crowe Ransom, *The World's Body* (New York, Charles Scribner's Sons, 1938).
32. See Austin Farrer, *The Glass of Vision* (Westminster, Dacre Press, 1948).

in a Time of Dearth

the philosophic enterprise itself (*pace* contemporary positivism) into a kind of poetry that it is extremely difficult, therefore, to identify clearly the precise difference being drawn between poet and thinker. Presumably, of course, the task of the thinker *qua* thinker is to win as large a competence as possible in supervising the procedures of discursive reason and dialectical argument; whereas the task of the poet *qua* poet is that of winning the greatest possible precision and resourcefulness in those ways of metaphor and analogy that are most distinctively native to the creative imagination. But, like the poet, the thinker, too, does not possess any legislative prerogatives in regard to primal reality. Systematic thought is bound to be something crippled and misshapen unless it originates in a "willingness . . . to be the enemy of nothing that is,—actual or possible, contingent or necessary, animate or inanimate, natural, human, or divine."[33] In the presence of Being, the attitude of both the poet and the thinker needs to be that of docility and submissiveness, for that very presence is itself a gift. Unless it is patiently hearkened to, in a spirit of acquiescence and gratitude, there can be no good result for either poetry or thought; for vision, whether poetic or metaphysical, requires that there be something to be seen—and something which we consent to be reached by, which we consent to accept as a gift.[34]

At whatever point Heidegger launches into an analysis of the nature of thought—whether in the essay *On the Essence of Truth*[35] (*Vom Wesen der Wahrheit*) or the Postscript to the essay *What is Metaphysics?*[36] (*Was ist Metaphysik?*) or the book of 1954, *Was heisst Denken*[37] (*What Evokes Thought*)—he is to be found stressing the impertinence of

33. Robert Jordan, "Poetry and Philosophy: Two Modes of Revelation," *Sewanee Review*, 67, no. 1 (January–March, 1959), p. 13.
34. Ibid.
35. Trans. R. F. C. Hull and Alan Crick, *Existence and Being*, pp. 319–51.
36. Ibid., pp. 355–92.
37. Tübingen, Niemeyer.

any attempt on the part of the thinker to seize reality by direct assault, since, before the thinker can even begin to undertake his various labors, he must wait for the advent of Being, for the advent of the Holy. Though this theme figures most immediately in Heidegger's meditations on the nature of the philosophic enterprise, it is yet so integral to the whole body of his thought, and the line of demarcation between poet and thinker is everywhere so lightly drawn in his work that we may, therefore, consider all that he has to say in this connection as bearing just as immediately on his theory of poetry as on his theory of the philosophic act itself. Both the poet and the thinker, in other words, are adepts in the art of paying heed to Being, and both, therefore, teach us something about what is involved in the discipline of waiting.

It is in the book of 1957, *Der Satz vom Grund*[38] (*The Principle of Ground*) and the book of 1959, *Gelassenheit* (recently translated into English under the title *Discourse on Thinking*), that Heidegger presents some of his most suggestive statements on this issue. Since everything that he says here about the thinker as one who waits pertains equally as much to his understanding of the poet, the appropriate transposition is to be made, as though it had been explicitly made by Heidegger himself.

The basic presupposition of the little book of 1959 is—as it is said by the Teacher in his conversation with the Scholar and the Scientist—that "We are to do nothing but wait."[39] And nothing else is to be done, since, in all our transactions with the world, what comes *to* us is not a *re*-presentation of something which has already emerged out of ourselves; indeed, to suppose the contrary to be the case is to have submitted all over again to the old wrongheadedness of attempting to "humanize" reality. The basic ontological situation is simply that of man-in-the-neighborhood-of-Being, and, since Being is not a human property at man's disposal, there is nothing to be done but tó await its coming-to-presence. And it is

38. Pfullingen, Neske.
39. *Discourse on Thinking*, p. 62.

just here that we may identify the nature of the discipline which the poet enjoins upon us; for it is a great part of his distinctive office to teach us how to wait, to teach us how to approach the environing reality of the world in a spirit of meditative openness—in the spirit of *Gelassenheit,* of surrender, of abandonment to the influxions of Being. The poet—that is, the artist in words, whether in verse or drama or prose fiction —so deploys his sounds and images and dramatic situations that we are compelled to recognize how gross and inadequate are the various concepts and counters with which we customarily order and interpret experience, and how reductive and distorting they often are of our actual life-world. Thus, in effect, he invites us, as we approach the world, to hold these concepts and counters in a state of suspension, to "leave open what we are waiting for,"[40] in order that our waiting may release itself into the openness of Being without violating that openness. This is indeed, for Heidegger, the true meaning of *Gelassenheit:* it consists in nothing other than our consenting to let things be and to dwell on the earth without restlessly searching all the time for ways of domesticating reality within a framework of human design and purpose.

Gelassenheit, in other words, is simply openness to the Mystery of Being. It is hinted in *Der Satz vom Grund* that, when *the will to will* in a man has been thus quietened and subdued, he may be found to be like that rose which is spoken of by the German mystical poet of the seventeenth century, Johannes Scheffler. Scheffler, generally known as Angelus Silesius (the name he gave himself after his conversion to the Roman Catholic Church), in one of the poems in his book *The Cherubinic Wanderer (Der Cherubinische Wandersmann)* declares:

> The rose is without why; it blooms because it blooms,
> It cares not for itself, asks not if it is seen.

This saying has very greatly fascinated Heidegger. For a rose that does not fret about the enabling conditions of its exist-

40. Ibid., p. 68.

81

ence, that is not constantly attacking the world and seeking to contain it within some scheme of concepts and categories, that simply blooms because it blooms, being quite content to be "without why"—such a rose, in its undemanding openness to the Mystery, to the Ground of Being, becomes for Heidegger a kind of sign, an emblem of what man himself is like when he is most truly human. Because—like the rose, he, too, if he is to be *gelassen* before the spectacle of the world and thus genuinely open to the influx of Being, must learn to bloom simply for the sake of blooming, must learn to live without "care," without predatoriness, without anxiety, "without why." Which is to say that he must learn how to wait, and even how to wait without needing to know precisely what it is he waits for; since, if we are to "abandon ourselves to the game"[41] of existence, we must make up our minds to the fact that there is no way of aprioristically charting and conceptualizing the miracle of Being. "We are to do nothing but wait." And this is the great lesson that we are taught by poetry.

So, in a way, we are brought back now to the scene that was being scanned in the previous chapter. Which is not, of course, to say, in the conceit that was there being employed, that Heidegger's is a position outside both Antioch and Alexandria. But what deserves to be remarked is that it is often to be found that such a position is that of many of the writers today who express in the most interesting ways a major strain of contemporary sensibility. What ought perhaps primarily to concern us is not so much the logic or illogic of that position itself but, rather, what it would appear most basically to be prompted by—namely, the conviction that the burdened and perplexed people of our age are best served by being invited, in a time of dearth, to be patient—and to wait.

Indeed, in many of the most representative plays and poems and novels of the immediate present, it is just at the point at which, apparently, 'a certain testimony is being tacitly made about waiting as the indispensable discipline to be undertaken

41. *Der Satz vom Grund*, p. 188.

by the human spirit in this late, bad time—it is just at this point that Martin Heidegger may be conceived to be the great philosophic master of the literary imagination in our period. And to remark his presence as that which looms massively behind much of contemporary literature is already perhaps to have a way of identifying what is most deeply problematic in that literature; for it is, I believe, precisely the large unanswered question raised by the craggy magnificence of Heidegger's vision that points toward what remains in doubt in the account being given now of our human estate by those artists whose work, in its relation to the soulscape of the age, seems most emphatically to be marked by "the tone of the center."

In the case of Heidegger, it is, I think we may say, the large element of gratuitousness in his piety that makes it something problematic. Surely it is a mode of piety that is chiefly expressed by the kind of meditation he has sustained over the last forty years. For here, in one who is perhaps the last great seer of modern philosophy, what seems most notable is the immense sensitivity of ecological conscience which prompts this thinker to regard the whole of reality as sacramental, in the sense that the true identity of everything that exists is considered to reside in its way of showing forth the Mystery of Being. Everything is, therefore, instinct with holiness; so the man who has a proper awareness of the sacramental character of the things of earth does not attack them, as if it were their final destiny simply to be dominated and raped by him. And he does not deal imperialistically with the world's resources, since he knows something like what Dylan Thomas says to be the case, that

> The force that through the green fuse drives the flower
> Drives my green age.
>
> . . .
>
> The force that drives the water through the rocks
> Drives my red blood.[42]

42. *The Collected Poems of Dylan Thomas* (New York, New Directions, 1953), p. 10.

To move down, in other words, into the deep inwardness of things is to know that they are not just so many dead appurtenances of the human enterprise but that they are, rather, awakened into reality by a presence—the presence of Being itself. Thus the things of earth are to be approached in a spirit of homage, not aggressively or exploitatively but reverently, since it is in them and through them that the advent of Being becomes manifest—to him who waits.

This is a style of imagination that unquestionably bespeaks a very profound kind of piety toward all the wondrous works of Creation—toward the outgoings of the morning and evening, toward the north and the south, toward the lion and the adder and the children of men, toward all the round world and they that dwell therein; for, in all this, if we consent patiently and reverently to wait, the advent of Being may be descried. Yet in the Heideggerian *pietas* there is unavoidably to be felt something gratuitous, since the docile reverence with which we are invited to await this advent could only be "proved" by some persuasive testimony that, when this advent comes, it will be found to bring an annunciation of something genuinely gracious—and, in behalf of such a possibility, Heidegger never submits any case.

If we undertake, then, to define what is ultimately problematic in Heidegger's whole vision, it must be said to be the large ambiguity that we are confronted by, when we find unanswered the question as to what it is in the character of Being that invites us, patiently and reverently (in Heidegger's sense of things), to await its advent. In this connection, it will be remembered with what stringency the late Albert Camus, in *Le Mythe de Sisyphe*, reproached those thinkers (like, as he felt, Kierkegaard and Chestov and Jaspers) who "leap" into metaphysical affirmativeness. And one suspects that, had he ever looked closely at the later Heidegger, this "poet" of Being would not altogether have escaped his severity, for Heidegger, too, is an athlete—who takes a great leap.

In suggesting that Martin Heidegger may be regarded as the philosophic master of that whole tendency in contemporary literature which is being reviewed in the previous chapter, I am not, of course, intending to imply that the specific themes of his thought have somehow made their way into the poetry and fiction and drama that most fully exemplify the period-style of the present time; for it is not at all such a relationship that he bears to this literature. What I would rather remark is that—whether one turns to the novels of Alain Robbe-Grillet and John Hawkes, or to the theatre of Beckett and Pinter, or to the poetry of Charles Olson and John Ashberry—our literature today, in its way of handling the human reality, seems often disinclined to accept the kind of large reconstructive effort so characteristic of traditionalist modernism. *Dans le Labyrinthe, The Crying of Lot 49, Krapp's Last Tape, Naked Lunch,* and *Les Nègres* belong to a new tradition deeply informed by a sense of the world as so radically contingent and indeterminate as to prevent the artist's doing anything other than simply offering an illustration of the chaos. It is a tradition that wants to forswear the old *profondeurs;* and thus it is a tradition that has tended to sponsor a kind of ethos in which the artist becomes a specialist in Hunger-Art, an adept in the art of doing without—of waiting (as the language of Eliot's "East Coker" puts it) "without hope," since any kind of hope at all would be hope for that for which the human experience offers no sanction in an age which is, as Heidegger says, "the No-more of the gods that have fled and the Not-yet of the god that is coming."

Such a waiting differs, to be sure, from Heidegger's, for his —given the vision of Being, the expectation of its advent—is a waiting attached to a very great hopefulness. Yet whether one waits, as in the case of Heidegger, with reverence and in hope, or whether, as in the case of the Beckett of *Fin de Partie,* one simply waits, it would seem that the logic of the case requires some antecedent assurance that that for which one waits will not be found in any way to be essentially spendthrift of the human spirit itself, an assurance that it is indeed in some sense really gracious, that it is worth waiting for. Yet the kind of waiting frequently connoted by the testimony of our new literature not only seems generally to lack the empowerment that such an assurance might provide but also seems often to lack even any real specificity of intent or clear destination. It is, in other words, a waiting unprepared to give any cogent account of itself, and thus, in its gratuitousness, we may feel Martin Heidegger to be its great philosophic scholiast. It is to be remembered, however, that this question as to what it means to wait has evoked still another body of contemporary testimony which is marked by that same austere religious grandeur so notably characteristic of Heidegger's meditations. It is indeed precisely "the ontology of the not yet" which constitutes the central issue of the massive and brilliant work of the distinguished East German Marxist philosopher Ernst Bloch, now living as an exile in West Germany. And I should not fail immediately to remark that my own misgivings about what is gratuitous in the kind of waiting enjoined today by the literary imagination would, in all likelihood, be responded to in an adverse way by Ernst Bloch, who would very probably assert that, in asking this waiting to clarify itself through some validating account of that for which it waits, I am in effect supposing that "confidence" is a necessary prerequisite for waiting. But, as he would doubtless argue, if one faces the future with confidence, then the future must itself be something already established and finished—in which case there can no longer be anything for which to wait.

In his great book of 1959, *Das Prinzip Hoffnung*, Bloch talks not about waiting but about hope, about that "infatuation with the possible" which he takes to be the basic principle of human existence and the fundamental theme for philosophic meditation. Man is indeed, in Bloch's anthropology, conceived to be a creature of hope, for he dwells interstitially—between what is and what is not yet, in the dimension of "not-yet-being" (*Noch-Nicht-Sein*). It is, in fact, just man's ineluctable orientation towards the future that leads Bloch, for all of his devotion to Feuerbach and Engels and Marx, very radically to revise the traditional Marxist critique of religion. He is himself, of course, an atheist who rejects any and every version of a substantialist metaphysical theism, with its vision of He-Who-Is; so it is not the *Deus absconditus*, it is not God, who lies ahead, and Bloch—unlike some of his theological disciples (say, the Germans Jürgen Moltmann and Wolfhart Pannenberg, or the American Harvey Cox)—does not want in any way theistically to conceive the idea of futurity; what lies ahead, indeed, is not the *Deus absconditus* but the *homo absconditus*. Nevertheless, he considers the real root of distinctively religious passion to be the longing for fulfillment, for "not-yet-being"—which leads, in St. Paul's phraseology, to "forgetting those things which are behind, and reaching forth unto those things which are before" (Philippians 3:13). However chimerical may be the anthropomorphic imagery whereby traditional theism objectifies the "things which are before," Bloch refuses to take the conventional Marxist line, that religion is simply a form of cultural pathology. In his hermeneutic, religion is hope —and hope originates in man's incorrigible fascination with the gap between what is and what is yet to be. So his is an "esoteric Marxism" which points toward "meta-religion."

Though Bloch's atheism is consistent and unremitting, his Principle of Hope, it is clear, does not refer to any particular finite projects or goals; it looks, rather, simply toward the "open space" of absolute futurity itself, towards that vacuum of "not-yet-being" which transcends all finite objectives, towards the unplumbable depths of *Noch-Nicht-Sein*. Yet, if it be suggested that steadily facing the openness of absolute futurity requires such an empowerment of the human spirit as can only be provided by the assurance that the future will itself be found in some way to be truly gracious—if it be suggested that waiting must, in the nature of the case, be grounded in faith, Bloch's immediate reply will be that hope is not "superstitious confidence."[43] Or, if it be asked what, then, it is that beckons the imagination out of the present and into the future, what it is that elicits hope, his answer will, in effect, be that hope posits itself and is grounded in nothing at

43. Ernst Bloch, *Das Prinzip Hoffnung* (Frankfurt am Main, Suhrkamp, 1959), p. 1523.

all resembling a *promissio Dei*, but simply in the boundless possibility represented by man's historical future. So, on this reckoning, it would seem that it would in fact be precisely the gratuitousness of that waiting which figures so much in the literary ethos of our period that authenticates the spirituality it expresses.

We are here, then, in a strange land indeed where the imagination appears—like the heroine of Gabriel Marcel's play *Le Monde cassé*—to be listening "into the void." But, as Lao Tzŭ reminds us, it is precisely the hole in the middle—"the space where there is nothing"—that makes the wheel.[44] And however gratuitous may seem a hearkening which is only to "the void," it may be that persistence in this mode of spirituality is, in our period, perhaps most especially for the artists of the word, the form which it is natural for the writer's fidelity to take—his fidelity, that is, to the uncreated Rock of reality. His business after all, as the English critic Frank Kermode has so finely said, "is not merely to satisfy the lovers of truth, but to make brilliant the poverty on which their thoughts dwell."[45] And in a time when to believe at all is, in Wallace Stevens' phrase, "to believe beyond belief," the poem will be

> the cry of its occasion,
> Part of the res itself and not about it.[46]

There is no way of guaranteeing, of course, that moving into the hole in the middle may prove to be a way of moving towards the wheel's periphery, but hoping that this may prove to be the case is, I believe, the central challenge presented to us by the literature of our time. For it is requiring us to explore anew, and deeply, the mystery of our privation and need— what Stevens called the mystery of "poverty."

44. Chap. 11 of *Tao Tê Ching*, trans. Arthur Waley in his *The Way and Its Power: A Study of the Tao Tê Ching and Its Place in Chinese Thought* (London, Allen and Unwin, 1934), p. 155.

45. Frank Kermode, *Wallace Stevens* (Edinburgh, Oliver & Boyd, 1960), p. 127.

46. Wallace Stevens, "An Ordinary Evening in New Haven," *Collected Poems*, p. 473.

Chapter Four POETRY
AND
PRAYER

Though most of the students who are working with me in the University of Chicago are engaged in interdisciplinary doctoral studies in theology and literature and are winning a fairly sophisticated awareness of the theoretical materials they need to be canvassing, I cannot recall having discovered any one of their number in recent years who, without having been told to do so, had felt the need to read the Abbé Henri Bremond's *Prière et Poésie*, or who indeed even evinced any sense of what still deserves to be considered impressive in this famous book. In this, I suppose these young people present a reflection of a generally prevalent attitude today of suspicion and indifference toward what is often referred to, in a tone of denigration, as "mystical aesthetic." However much in certain respects the Romantic dispensation may have persisted on into the Age of Eliot, its cult of inspiration, its doctrine of transport, the whole machinery of what is popularly considered to be its characteristic *frisson*, has lost its appeal for contemporary taste. The line of thinking about poetry anciently expressed in the *Ion* and the *Peri Hupsous* and reiterated in the modern period by the English and German Romantics is regarded as making for a kind of inflationary effusiveness that brings genuine reflection to a halt. Thus whatever is to be found trenching on a poetics of Elevation and the Sublime is given a very hard time by the reigning schools of our period.

As Jacques Maritain was at pains to remind us, however,

in his Mellon Lectures in the early '50s, this strain of vigorous anti-Romanticism in modern theory of literature has in fact entailed a mystique of its own. For the eagerness of an earlier generation to regard poetry as an affair of transport and exaltation has in our time simply been replaced by an equally great eagerness to regard it as merely an affair of *operation* in which artists function only as "engineers in the manufacturing of an artifact of words or sounds."[1] And this antiseptic reduction is not without its own obscurantism.

Yet, for all of our great inclination today toward austerity in the conception of the poem and the poet's vocation, when I do succeed in persuading my own graduate students (or—as they might prefer to have it put—in gently coercing them) to read Henri Bremond, the experience that I occasionally have is that of feeling that they, on putting down *Prière et Poésie*, have felt that at least the Abbé was perhaps the most distinguished of Longinus' modern epigones and that *something* important is at least being adumbrated in this book. It will, of course, be remembered that the line taken is one which insists on the essentially mystical character of poetic apprehension: it is argued that the inherent dynamism of the poetic mind necessarily drives it toward a state of prayer from which the poet turns away only in order to complete the labor of composition itself. The excitement to which poetic art conduces is the excitement of a mystical experience that has not discovered itself to be what in point of fact it really is and that does not, therefore, go on to allow the contemplative impulse to complete itself in an act of mergence with the Divine Ground. The poetic transaction, in other words, belongs to a secondary order of mystical experience—secondary, that is, because it does not, characteristically, culminate in the Beatific Vision. Yet, even so, the Abbé contended, this is an order of experience whose nature it is to afford a kind of radically intuitive penetration of reality that is essentially akin to mystical apprehension and that would indeed, if given full play, develop into a truly mystical

---

1. Jacques Maritain, *Creative Intuition in Art and Poetry*, p. 62.

sentiency. In short, the inherent thrust of the poetic experience propels it toward Transcendence, and its end is prayer and the soul's enjoyment of the Divine Presence. This is, in general, the contour belonging to the argument of this famous book. But the argument, in its detail, is not, of course, itself any longer felt to carry a cogency that is altogether compelling and persuasive (though, of its sort, it is perhaps, in Bremond's exposition, the major modern instance). In the first place, simply at the level of what is implied for theory of literature, what is most troubling about the doctrine of *Prière et Poésie* is its tendency to dissolve the objective reality of works of literary art into a particular kind of eidetic consequence to which, presumably, they conduce. What is being promoted, in effect, is a basic shift of the center of poetic theory from the poem to its results, and the error here is that which W. K. Wimsatt and Monroe Beardsley have taught us to understand as exemplifying the Affective Fallacy—which is fallacious because it refocuses aesthetic discussion away from those norms of corrigibility resident in the work of art itself and attempts to base it on various unadjudicable subjective meanings.[2] The essential logic of Bremond's position, in other words, is not calculated to accord due recognition to those values in literature that are inherent and terminal; it sanctions our paying serious attention to literature only in so far as it can be determined to have certain nonliterary consequences. Which is to say that, finally, the Abbé shows himself (in paraphrase of T. S. Eliot's famous dictum) to have been interested in considering poetry not as poetry but as another thing, or as the occasion or stimulus for another thing.

Nor can one feel that anything at all is gained in clarity by thinking of the poet as characterized primarily by a certain expertness in *vision;* for surely he is, first of all, a certain kind of maker. The Abbé liked to suppose that "the more of a poet

2. See W. K. Wimsatt, Jr., and Monroe C. Beardsley, "The Affective Fallacy," *The Sewanee Review,* 57 (Winter 1949). This essay is reprinted in Professor Wimsatt's *The Verbal Icon: Studies in the Meaning of Poetry* (Lexington, University of Kentucky Press, 1954).

any particular poet is, the more he is tormented by the need of communicating his experience"—which provoked T. S. Eliot's delightfully tart rejoinder that, on the contrary, "the poet is tormented primarily by the need to write a poem"[3] (as indeed "are a legion of people who are not poets"[4]).

Finally, it would also seem that the issue involving the relation of *poiesis* to religious experience requires definition in terms of an infinitely greater tact than Henri Bremond managed to summon. For, as Rosalind Murray has reminded us, the poet "is in fact never saying: 'Speak, Lord, for Thy servant heareth,' but always 'Tell me something that I can make use of!' "[5] Which is to say that art is a productive activity, a virtue of the practical intellect—and, as such, it is concerned to fashion (and to discover) an order amidst the rich and enigmatic heterogeneity of the created world. Whereas, that more final quest of

> knowledge through connaturality which is peculiar to mystical experience comes about either, in natural mystical experience, by means of merely intellectual concentration producing a void through which the Self is ineffably touched or, in grace-given mystical experience, by means of charity, which connatures the soul with God, and which transcends both emotion and the human recesses of the subjectivity. Poetic experience is from the very start oriented toward expression, and terminates in a word uttered, or a work produced; while mystical experience tends toward silence, and terminates in an immanent frution of the absolute.[6]

Yet, however much the Abbé Henri Bremond's formulation may need to be corrected and revised, he has by no means stood alone in supposing that there is a periphery of experience on which poetry does crucially touch the life of prayer.

3. T. S. Eliot, *The Use of Poetry and the Use of Criticism* (London, Faber and Faber, 1934), p. 138.
4. Ibid.
5. Rosalind Murray, *The Forsaken Fountain* (London, Hollis and Carter, 1948), p. 91.
6. Jacques Maritain, pp. 234–35.

And we ought not to be dissuaded from freshly attempting to think the issue through by the almost habitual tendency of those who have previously contemplated it to become entangled in something like the Abbé's confusions.

It ought, of course, first of all to be understood that, most especially if the materials of modern literature are in view, it will not be profitable for us to restrict the scope of poetry to those forms of verbal art which employ the techniques of verse. In his book *The Arts of the Beautiful*, M. Gilson offers, somewhat confusedly, a recent statement of the conventional notion that there is some uniquely close connection between verse and "beauty" in the arts of the word and that metered expression is the natural medium of poetry.[7] But, as Edmund Wilson reminded us many years ago in an extraordinarily perceptive essay in *The Triple Thinkers*, the plain fact of the matter is that the time has come "to discard the word 'poetry' or to define it in such a way as to take account of the fact that the most intense, the most profound, the most beautifully composed and the most comprehensive of the great works of literary art . . . have been written sometimes in verse technique, sometimes in prose technique, depending partly on the taste of the author, partly on the mere current fashion."[8] And, as he said, "If, in writing about 'poetry,' one limits oneself to 'poets' who compose in verse, one excludes too much of modern literature"[9]—as, for example, that crucial river scene in *The Ambassadors* in which Strether suddenly discerns the true relationship between Chad and Mme. de Vionnet, or the *Anna Livia Plurabelle* "canto" of *Finnegans Wake*, or the account of the last desperate winter, amid the icy wastes of Yuriatin, that Yurii Andreievich and Larisa have together in *Zhivago*, or the colloquies between Gogo and Didi in *Godot*, or the climactic scene in *Mutter Courage*, in which the Mother

7. See Etienne Gilson, *The Arts of the Beautiful* (New York, Charles Scribner's Sons, 1965), chap. 4.
8. Edmund Wilson, "Is Verse a Dying Technique?" *The Triple Thinkers* (New York, Oxford University Press, 1948), p. 21.
9. Ibid., p. 25.

sits humped over the dead Kattrin, and so on and on and on.
It seems sensible, therefore, when one uses the term "poetry,"
to mean simply all the high forms of literature that make fictions in such a way as to invite the mind to gaze, with radical
amazement, into the depth of the human mystery.

When the poetic enterprise is understood, then, to have
this kind of spaciousness of scope and possibility, in what respects may it be considered to represent a singular employment of the imagination? This is a question that has, I think,
been most cogently answered in that tradition of late Kantian
thought which, in recent speculation, is perhaps most impres-
sively represented by such thinkers as Ernst Cassirer, Wilbur
Marshall Urban, Susanne Langer, and Philip Wheelwright.
In this line of modern aesthetic, poetry, and the arts generally,
are regarded as one of the great ways whereby the imagination
reaches "intentively" beyond the immediate givens of experience (as it also does in scientific pursuits), and does so by way
of contemplating what these givens may symbolize or mean.
Man, as Cassirer liked to say, is the *animal symbolicum*.[10] He
does not merely receive various kinds of challenge and in-
ducement from his external environment and then react to
them; his experience is not wholly, or even most basically,
contained within the functional circle of stimulus-and-re-
sponse; he lives in the new dimension of what Mrs. Langer
calls "symbolic transformation."[11] He does not live simply in
"a world of hard facts, or according to his immediate needs
and desires,"[12] but always in the midst of the sciences, arts,
myths, and religions whereby the data of immediate experience are wrought into the significant forms that the mind requires for its sanity and peace.

It is the mistaken tendency, however, of the reigning school
in Anglo-American philosophy today to suppose that reality

10. Ernst Cassirer, *An Essay on Man* (Garden City, Doubleday [An-
chor Books], 1953), p. 44.
11. See Susanne K. Langer, *Philosophy in a New Key* (New York,
Penguin Books, 1948), chap. 2.
12. Ernst Cassirer, p. 43.

is handled with genuine precision and seriousness only by those modes of symbolization that are susceptible of being authenticated by controlled experiments of an empirical order. Discursive symbolism alone is considered to be capable of providing vehicles for thought, and truth is not regarded as a possible property of those nondiscursive types of symbolic form that are so much of the essence of all artistic and religious expression. The common supposition is that, in regard to what is "really" the case, a pointer reading of some sort represents a kind of symbolic form that has a truly referential capacity; whereas a work of poetic art or a prayer, however fascinating it may be to study the special "language game" involved, need not be expected to afford insight into anything other than the particular style of imagination of which it is an expression.

The denial of any ontological intention to those forms of symbolic action characteristic of poetic art has doubtless in part been encouraged by that modern apologetic for poetry which descends from the Symbolists and which so radically asserts the autonomousness of the poetic universe as in effect to close off all avenues leading from it to the outside world. But this doctrine is itself an exacerbated response to the more fundamental and the more pervasive modern attitude of skepticism about the dignity of any cognitive pretension that may be made by the various nonscientific types of symbolic discourse. For, in a culture so riddled as our own with the disease of positivism, the most natural assumption is that the order which science seeks in the world is that in terms of which alone it is possible to harmonize the significant realities of human existence.

Yet, the satisfaction which we continue to derive from the highly complicated systems of utterance and discourse that comprise the various forms of literary art is surely a persisting attestation to the possibility of our taking hold of What Is[13] by methods other than those of empirical science. And what

13. This usage is Philip Wheelwright's; see his *Metaphor and Reality* (Bloomington, Indiana University Press, 1962), p. 30 and passim.

is, of course, decisive here is the great need that we have to pay attention to, even to revel in, the raw concreteness of things—and the unavailability for this purpose of any other symbolic stratagems except those which art employs. The fact of the matter is that the human spirit simply cannot dwell habitually in that "system of all-inclusive relations" which is what the universe was declared to be by the distinguished British Hegelian of the last century, T. H. Green. One of man's deepest yearnings is to savor, in the full flavor of their richly existential particularity, the immediate givens that constitute the furniture and environment of his living. And it is only by way of a living confrontation with the full-fledged otherness of the things of this world—its people, its events, its natural realities and processes—that there can ever be borne in upon us that awareness apart from which we are not fully human, of being placed in a universe whose ontological amplitude does not already lie within the depths of man himself but entails, rather, dimensions of Transcendence that hint at "unknown modes of Being."

Both science and art bring into play activities of the mind that involve its mingling with the circumambient world, but the scientific employments of reason entail a certain principled impatience with the raggedly concrete and individual aspects of reality. What matters, in the perspective of science, is not the radical singularity of particular things and events but the logical relations and the general laws that are instanced in particular cases. Aristotle puts the matter in this way in the *Posterior Analytics* (87b,28): "Perception must be of a particular, whereas scientific knowledge involves the recognition of the commensurate universal." Thus he very nicely expresses the ineradicable bias of scientific mentality—which does not linger upon singulars and which is always baffled until it finds universals. This is of the very essence of its peculiar asceticism. Scientific mentality assumes that no significantly veridical information about the world can be derived from a contemplation of the particular event, the unrepeatable experience, the unique reality; so it is always withdrawing from particular

realities in order to get to the universal rules which they may
be taken to exhibit or confirm; and it is happy only when it
reaches that region of unresisting generalities which can, completely and without remainder, be subdued by the abstractive
intellect.

Indeed, it is this rigorous asceticism of scientific mentality
that doubtless accounts for the suspiciousness with which it
has perennially viewed the arts, and most especially the poetic
arts. For poetry is a virtue of that "intransitive attention"[14]
which is bestowed on the quiddity and what Scotus called the
"hecceity" (i.e., the sheer "thisness") of things. The catharsis
which it brings is simply the profound relief that is enjoyed
by the mind when, in being offered a chance to luxuriate in
the contemplation of the intractable givenness and particularity of individual existents, it wins some surety that its scope
is larger than its own brainpan. The poet—that is, the artist in
language, whatever may be his particular genre—does not,
characteristically, bring the abstractive passion of science,
and its universalizing perspectives, to his dealings with the
world; he consents to allow what is irregular and nonconform-
ist and unique to have a very sharp impact upon him, and he
does not spirit it away into any "system of all-inclusive relations." He wants to apprehend that irreducible particularity of
a thing whereby it is what it is instead of being a thousand
other possible things.

Poetry is, in short, forever fascinated with what is radically
specific and individual—with the brooding, eerie gloom of *this*
lonely heath (as in Hardy's *The Return of the Native*), with the
unhinging fright of *this* young soldier before the advance to
the front (as in Crane's *The Red Badge of Courage*), with the
"dooms of love" through which *my* father moved (as in E. E.
Cummings' great elegy). Richard Wilbur, for example, sees

14. The term "intransitive attention" is used by Eliseo Vivas to define
the chief differentia of the aesthetic experience. It is, he says, an experience of "intransitive attention"; see his "A Definition of the Aesthetic
Experience," *Creation and Discovery: Essays in Criticism and Aesthetics*
(New York, Noonday Press, 1955), pp. 93–99.

"a landscapeful of small black birds . . . convene at some command . . . in the middle of the air"; and, then, they are gone, rolling "like a drunken fingerprint across the sky"—shattering and maddening ". . . space/With their divergences." And, as he says,

> Delighted with myself and with the birds,
> I set them down and give them leave to be.
> It is by words and the defeat of words,
> Down sudden vistas of the vain attempt,
> That for a flying moment one may see
> By what cross-purposes the world is dreamt.[15]

His poem is called "An Event"—and it is precisely in terms of such singularity as this that the poet normally finds his "glass of vision" wherewith to "see/By what cross-purposes the world is dreamt."

It is Gerard Manley Hopkins who gives us one of the great renderings in modern theory of this unshakeable commitment which poetry has to the rich unicity of the concrete singular. In the period following his years at Oxford, as he was working out his basic understanding of what is distinctively characteristic of the *via poetica*, he found his thought more and more to be centralized in two concepts which, in terms of his own coinage, are designated as "inscape" and "instress." Even after the most careful rummaging through his *Papers*, it is difficult to be certain that one has altogether got right his exact intention in regard to the meaning of these terms. "Inscape" naturally implies a contrast between itself and "landscape," and one supposes that Hopkins meant it to suggest not an outer reality, not something necessarily and unevadably present, but something that is discoverable only by the most tactful penetration into the inwardness of the things of earth— that essential design which constitutes intrinsic form. By "instress" he seems to have meant that energy of being whereby a thing manages to be what it is. He assumed, as he said, that

15. Richard Wilbur, "An Event," *Things of This World*, p. 46.

"mere possibility, passive power, is not power proper and has no activity": "it cannot of itself come to stress, cannot instress itself."[16] In order for a thing to be "upheld,"[17] it must be imbued with a perfection of being sufficient to enable it to maintain its actuality. The instress of a given reality, in other words, is that power by which its inscape is held together: as one sees into a thing, it is that ontological potency which one feels to be the essential ground of the basic design, that principle of enablement whereby it is what it is, rather than another thing. Instress might, indeed, be said to be the "cause" of inscape. As Hopkins said in his letter of February 15, 1879, to Robert Bridges, "as air, melody, is what strikes me most of all in music and design in painting, so design, pattern or what I am in the habit of calling 'inscape' is what I above all aim at in poetry."[18]

The Roman statesman and monk of the sixth century, Cassiodorus, declared, "God is really wonderful and extremely wise in having distinguished every one of his creatures by a unique dispensation lest unseemly confusion overwhelm them."[19] And it is indeed this unique dispensation, this inscape, in things to which it is the principal responsibility of poetry to pay attention. Its love affair, as Hopkins said, is with "the particularity of each unique thing as observed," and it wants to notice and to look at all the "hecceities" that come our way.

Though poetry addresses itself to the radically singular, concrete, individual aspects of reality, it has perennially been the wisdom of those who have reflected upon it most deeply (ever since Aristotle) to discern that, though it begins with the singular rather than the universal, it ends by somehow pre-

16. *The Note-Books and Papers of Gerard Manley Hopkins*, ed. Humphry House, p. 310.

17. Ibid., p. 98.

18. *The Letters of Gerard Manley Hopkins to Robert Bridges*, ed. C. C. Abbott (London and New York, Oxford University Press, 1935), p. 66.

19. Quoted in Philip Wheelwright, *The Burning Fountain: A Study in the Language of Symbolism* (Bloomington, Indiana University Press, 1954), pp. 78–79.

senting both, by treating the singular in such a way that it becomes a glass of vision through which the universal may be seen. This is doubtless what Whitehead meant when he remarked somewhere that "Art at its highest exemplifies the metaphysical doctrine of the interweaving of absoluteness upon relativity." The compelling power of "things" to command the poet's attention flows from the relationships that the things exemplify and bespeak. Indeed, the things which poetry handles, though separate and distinct, are (as Father McCarron was reminding us many years ago in his fine little book *Realization*) "interacting as in a story or fragment of a story. Such action upon one another is the evidence of their interrelationship."[20] And, were it not for this interrelationship amongst things, poetry would be impossible. Nothing that exists is an island unto itself; or, to change the metaphor, everything that holds membership in the world is an element of a seamless garment—the "ragged edges" of every individual reality splay off onto those of another, and "the world is a wedding." Day Lewis reminds us that "if we shoot a bird, we wound ourselves,"[21] and Wordsworth was often wanting us to remember that

> dark
> Inscrutable workmanship that reconciles
> Discordant elements, makes them cling together
> In one society.

So, since any point which, from a certain angle of vision, may be seen to be a center is likely, from another perspective, to be found to be on the periphery of still another center, the poet is bound to find—and does in fact always find—that his concrete singular, when faced with great intensity, "without losing any of its bright actuality, tends also to be, or at least

20. Hugh McCarron, *Realization: A Philosophy of Poetry* (London, Sheed and Ward, 1937), p. 73.
21. C. Day Lewis, *The Poetic Image* (London, Jonathan Cape, 1947), p. 33.

to suggest overtones of, something more."[22] It becomes what Hegel called a "concrete universal." And it is the habit that poetic art has of dwelling upon the interrelationships, the clusters of analogy among things, that makes it essentially symbolic. It wants to show how deeply resemblance and analogy are characteristic of reality itself; it wants to show how miraculously the concrete individual, when steadily contemplated, opens out into a kind of infinite depth and extension, so that its ultimate significance is discerned to flow from relations in which it stands to still other things consubstantial with itself. Thus, as Coleridge was insisting in the *Biographia Literaria*, the poet does not see reality as "essentially fixed and dead" but as "essentially vital." His great commitment, to be sure, is to the individual fact; yet it is not the mere fact that captivates him, but the concrete singular as it is itself ignited by such a power of reciprocity as permits it to trench upon still other realities, so that it takes on the luster of a "something more." This is why indeed synecdoche and metaphor— whether in verse, drama, or fiction—are so much of the essence of poetic art, for the poet's final intention is to produce such a "coalescence"[23] of the heterogeneities of experience as will evoke in us some awareness of the vitally fluid unity of the world and thus offer a kind of attestation to an infinitude beyond "the light of sense."

The ontological dimension, in other words, to which poetic experience belongs is the dimension of depth. For the strange greatness of the poet's task—of a Shakespeare, a Melville, a Tolstoi, an Eliot—involves his effort, through all the marvelous cunning of his craft, to arrange for another visitation being paid us by the concrete realities of our world (many of them long since familiar)—and one that will stir us into fresh apprehension of how really inexhaustible in fact they are. Is it

22. Philip Wheelwright, *Metaphor and Reality*, p. 167.
23. Ibid., pp. 164–69; "coalescence," as a feature of the world when beheld in the terms of poetic vision, is analyzed by Professor Wheelwright in these pages with a marvelous sensitiveness and tact.

not the case, for example, that Shakespeare's Lear, Melville's Ahab, Tolstoi's Anna, and the dramatic actions of which they are a part testify, as it were, to the infinite depth and the radical mysteriousness of the human reality in the very disclosures that they bring to us of what is recalcitrantly finite in the world of the human creature? Or, to think of what is quite a different sort of case, it ought not to be any great occasion of astonishment that his early admiration of the poet of *Une Saison en Enfer* should have been found by Paul Claudel to be a kind of *preparatio* in his own life for a deeper entrance into the Christian faith; for, despite all the violence of spirit and all the blasphemy that are expressed in Rimbaud's poetry, here at least one encounters a sense of the abysses encircling human life that might indeed well lead to a deeper seizure of a Gospel of Grace. Or, again, to move from the vertiginous Inferno of Rimbaud to the arcadian countryside of Robert Frost's New England, one feels even in something so apparently simple and earthbound as Frost's "Stopping By Woods on a Snowy Evening" that curious metaphysical vastness and resonance which are so much the hallmarks of great poetry. Even when the frame of reference is of so limited a sort as in Frost's brief lyric, the poet, in the degree to which he has entered into a real engagement with his medium and the world that presses in upon him, is attempting to intensify our experiential encounter with whatever segment of reality it may be that has laid hold of his imagination. And the miracle that is so much of the essence of the poetic process grows out of the fact that the more profoundly the poet realizes and renders his "inscape" the more it tends to "point beyond itself, or rather, points to unplumbed and unplumbable depths within itself."[24] It becomes vocal, it attains the power of "speaking" to us, and thus we are introduced into the order of what Gabriel Marcel calls Presence, there where reality is encountered in its dimension of depth, of inexhaustibility, of radical mystery. Here it is that we feel ourselves "spoken" to by the deep things of

24. Theodore M. Greene, "The Ontological Dimension of Experience," *Thought*, 29, no. 114 (Autumn 1954), 374.

ourselves and our world, as though they were but a taproot uniting the human reality with the ultimate Ground of all reality.

It is, I believe, in some such way as this that poetic experience is suffused, in its intensest modes, with an awareness of the world, in its concrete phenomenality, as a sacrament of the divine immanence. And, of course, to be in the situation of beholding the world in its dimension of depth and to know ourselves searched and "spoken" to by that depth is very nearly to be in the situation of prayer; for prayer is nothing but the most cruelly delusive autosuggestion, if it be not a heedless exposure of ourselves to what is ultimately Deep in the common, ordinary, concrete realities of our experience. Catholic Christianity, in its Roman, Orthodox, and Anglican forms, has produced a literature of manuals on "the spiritual life" that is now so large as doubtless to be a cause of catalogic despair to the curators of theological libraries. And surely most of this literature, in our late stage of things, ought to begin to receive a very stringent reassessment, if for no other reason than that the very concept of "the spiritual life"—in the sense of a space apart from our normal daily habitat, a "religious quarter"—is, as Bishop Robinson has reminded us, most profoundly unbiblical.[25] As that good Scotsman of the Iona Community, George Macleod, bids us to realize,

> What debilitates our prayer life . . . is our presupposition that the pressures of life are on one side while God is on some other side: interested and concerned but on some other side. With this supposition, when evening comes with an ending to our pressures, we are apt to go eagerly to God —disconcertingly to find a vacuum. We seek to fill the vacuum with "spiritual thoughts." The more we try the more desperate does the situation become: till in effect we say that we are not really the praying type. Thus we begin to lean perilously to one side of the knife-edge.

25. John A. T. Robinson, *Honest to God* (Philadelphia, Westminster Press, 1963), p. 102.

There are, of course, evenings when our prayer-life is refreshing: but, analysed, they turn out to be the times when the pressures have been so weighty that you have simply had to go with them to God. But this precisely is the recovery of the knife-edge.[26]

Dr. Macleod's intention is to assert what any robust Christianity must surely need to assert, that the place of prayer is, most essentially, not what traditional spirituality calls "the interior life" but the Emmaus Road, not at the edges of life but in the midst of it, where all the pressures of the human reality are felt with greatest intensity. As that remarkable young German Protestant theologian, Dietrich Bonhoeffer, was declaring so movingly just before his martyrdom on a Nazi scaffold at the close of World War II, the life of the Christian man is a "worldly" life.[27] And this, I am proposing, is where it is the special concern of great literature to take us—back into the world, and into those deeper places of it, where the existential reality takes on the character of a threshold, becoming "the borderland of a something more."[28]

It ought not to be supposed, however, most especially where the characteristic literature of the modern period is in view, that there is any *scala sacra* affording a simple and direct ascent from poetry to prayer—and, in so far as the Abbé Henri Bremond's formulations tend to encourage this expectation, it may be just in this respect that they lead to the greatest confusion. Ours is, of course, a literature that has deeply involved itself in all those questions with which it has traditionally been the office of religious faith to deal; but it has done so generally in a spirit of resistance and even of competition, so far as the great traditions of Christian belief are concerned. When we put ourselves in mind of such artists as Kafka, Rilke, Lawrence, Gide, and Brecht, it does indeed seem that the modern

26. George Macleod, *Only One Way Left* (Glasgow, Iona Community, 1956), p. 160.
27. See Dietrich Bonhoeffer, *Letters and Papers from Prison*, trans. Reginald Fuller and ed. Eberhard Bethge (London, S.C.M. Press, 1953).
28. Philip Wheelwright, *The Burning Fountain*, p. 8.

and Prayer

writer has been taking "a swarm of spears into his breast" and fighting through all the issues of the age without any adventitious aids or supports at all.[29] When you are dealing with *Death in Venice, The Castle,* the *Duino Elegies,* and the late poems of Yeats, you are dealing with a literature that manifests a most intense concern with the whole issue of what in the language of religion is called salvation. "Its purpose," as remarked by one commentator, "is to trouble and upset us, to make us doubt the value of those things which our parents, and all of respectable society, taught us we were to be most sure of. More than the secular literature of any other time . . . modern literature reaches into our most private selves,"[30] in its effort to discover what it means to be human in this late, bad time. Thus one cannot but be struck by the absurdity of the judgment expressed many years ago by Ortega in his famous essay *The Dehumanization of Art,* in which he declared that modern literature was progressively moving away from the human; for this, surely, as a basic thesis about the poetry, fiction, and drama of the twentieth century, is quite indefensible. Indeed, it may well be that no other body of literature has been so extreme and so explicit in its concern with the human situation. It is in fact a literature that, in the most decisive way, asks us to deal with doctrine, and with the hardest kind of doctrine—that which has to do with the nature of ourselves. And what in part makes its doctrine about the human story so notable is the very radical kind of independence that it exhibits vis-à-vis the established traditions of Christian belief.

It is natural in our time, though, to take for granted a kind of tension between Christianity and the poetic imagination not only because of the extreme autonomy that, morally and religiously, the modern writer has often laid claim to. What is also at issue here is the sharp divergence from traditional

29. See Amos N. Wilder, *Modern Poetry and the Christian Tradition,* p. 196.
30. Lionel Trilling, "Commitment to the Modern," *Teachers College Record,* 64, no. 5 (February 1963), 405–06.

105

Christian perspectives of the very negative vision of the human prospect that has been generally characteristic of our literature. In the representative expressions of our period-style —in the poetry of Ezra Pound and Gottfried Benn; in the theatre of Brecht, Beckett, and Ionesco; in the fiction of Kafka, Sartre, Robbe-Grillet, and John Hawkes—the human image that is projected is something like those doomed ghosts in the pictures of the contemporary English painter Francis Bacon, who look out at the world heart-stricken and aghast; or it is like a face described by the English writer Alex Comfort in his novel *On This Side Nothing:* "I saw the same fear in her face that I should have felt if a stranger called at night, the worldwide twentieth-century fear which one sees wherever one knocks unexpectedly at any door."

Indeed, all those writers who are today rendering experience in the classic modern idioms are forging an image of the human creature as one ousted from the precincts of security and grace—as one who has no place of safety and whose being is therefore "porous . . . like those cryptic human figures in modern sculpture that are full of holes or gaps."[31] The German philosopher, Helmut Kuhn, several years ago entitled his study of Existentialism *Encounter With Nothingness,* and it would be difficult to come by any other phrase that so concisely renders the spiritual drama that is enacted in much of the representative literature of our period. The protagonists in these records of modern sensibility are creatures "full of holes and gaps, faceless, riddled with doubts and negations, starkly finite"[32]—and, in their porousness, they are at the point of being invaded by the surrounding Nothingness. Perhaps the ideogram most perfectly depicting the human presence which this literature portrays is the cipher.

This sense of man's impoverishment and indigence that so deeply informs a widely prevalent mood today does not, of course, spring from any merely willful inclination toward

31. William Barrett, *Irrational Man: A Study in Existential Philosophy* (Garden City, Doubleday, 1958), p. 54.
32. Ibid., p. 57.

Manichaean styles of imagination. It is rather doubtless in part a consequence of our feeling overwhelmed by the ambiguous results of our own creativity. By virtue of the political and scientific instrumentalities that we have fashioned, we find ourselves living in a world whose potential explosiveness infinitely surpasses any of the dangers that in one period or another have figured in man's recorded past. And, in this perilous time, there has arisen—and naturally so—a crisis of confidence in our ability to manage the arena of history. In the presence of a scientific establishment that has ushered in the nuclear age and in the presence of a political establishment that generates so much frightening tension in the world community, we feel that—like Mary Shelley's Frankenstein—we may have created a "second nature" which is beyond our capacity to control. Far more profoundly even, the sense of human life as totally contingent and as therefore exposed to the invading pressures of Nothingness is today a result of that general collapse of confidence in the cogency of traditional religious faith which undoubtedly constitutes the basic loss that underlies all the other losses that are felt by the men and women of our age.

However one accounts, though, for what is presently negative in the human image that drifts throughout the literature of our time, its bleakness cannot be gainsaid and does in fact bespeak a vision of man which is very sharply divergent from that which is proposed by the Christian Gospel. For, far from being any kind of faceless cipher, man is disclosed in the Christian story about reality to be a creature "trailing clouds of glory." In the perspectives of biblical thought, the "glory" of God is that power, that creative energy, by which whatever exists is called into existence; and man is declared to be made in the image of this glory. Which is to say that he is a radically theological being; he is "open" to the ineffable mystery of the Ground of Being; the light of his being is (as it is so beautifully said by Hans Urs von Balthasar)[33] "a dialogical

33. Hans Urs von Balthasar, *Science, Religion and Christianity*, trans. Hilda Graef (Westminster, Md., Newman Press, 1958), p. 49.

light," for, in the basic constitution of his nature, he is turned toward God, and—in Christian experience—the God whom he meets is turned toward him. But, though "trailing clouds of glory," man is yet, in the Christian sense of things, known to be essentially a creature. He must have air to breathe; he needs space in which to abide; if he cannot find warmth and nourishment, he will perish; yet, even with plentifulness of what are called "creature comforts," his life is but of short duration— and though we sing in our chains like the sea, said Dylan Thomas, Time holds us green and dying.[34] Our lives are embedded not only in the contingencies of nature but also in the relativities of history, since our perspectives are always partial and conditioned by the particular time and place that we happen to occupy. Yet, though man is a creature, "the fact that, through reason and memory and imagination, he can surmount himself and his world indeterminately means that his life cannot find its true ground in any of the proximate norms that emerge out of historical experience, and that he is therefore driven by the inner dynamism of his nature toward a transcendent norm."[35] He is, in short, open to God, or, as it is said in the very drastic language of the Bible, he is made "in the image of God" (Gen 1:26). Which is to say that we do indeed (as St. Paul puts it) "reflect as in a mirror the splendour of the Lord; [and] thus we are transfigured into his likeness, from splendour to splendour" (II Cor 3:18; N.E.B. trans.)— "from glory to glory." To be human is, in short, in the Christian sense of reality, to be stamped by and to bear the imprint in oneself of the glory of God.

This is, however, a way of thinking about human existence that differs most sharply from the sense of things that tends generally to be expressed in the literature of our time. Thus, from one standpoint, it might well be expected that those representing Christian perspectives would face this literature with

34. I have paraphrased the last two lines of Thomas' "Fern Hill"; see Dylan Thomas, *Collected Poems*, p. 180.
35. Nathan A. Scott, Jr., *Reinhold Niebuhr* (Minneapolis, University of Minnesota Press, 1963), p. 22.

a good deal of suspiciousness and hostility. Yet this need not be the case, and, indeed, in my judgment, it ought not to be the case; for the Christian man cannot reasonably expect the artist to do impossibles. The plain fact of the matter is that for perhaps the great majority of men today in the Western world there has occurred a profound erosion of the terrain of religious faith. Nor is this something which the Christian man confronts externally, for, in so far as he breathes the atmosphere of our age, he is himself in some sort a secular man. Thus it is that many of the most sensitive theologians of our period—Protestants like the late Paul Tillich and the late Dietrich Bonhoeffer, Roman Catholics like Karl Rahner and Hans Urs von Balthasar, Anglicans like John Robinson and Paul Van Buren—thus it is that they, in one way or another, are brooding upon the "eclipse" of God, or the "absence" of God. It is indeed something like this that constitutes a primary datum for the religious imagination in our time, since men whose standards of intelligibility derive from a world of electric lights and telephones and nuclear fission are not certain now as to how it is that we may continue any longer to speak of God and of Transcendence. Where is the "place," to speak metaphorically—where is the place in which God may be said to be? This will, increasingly, for contemporary theology be the central question to be anxiously wrestled with.

We have, all of us, so to speak, "fallen" into the Profane, and the historian of religion Mircea Eliade suggests that "desacralization" is the category that most comprehensively describes the spiritual situation of modern man.[36] So our literature, if it is to be an authentically contemporary literature, will inevitably be secular, and the world which it describes will be a world in which God appears in some way to have disappeared. And not only will ours be a secular literature, but I would myself hope that it would be radically secular, since skepticism and negation and denial may, if they are profound enough, by reason of their very radicalism, begin to quicken

36. See Mircea Eliade, *Birth and Rebirth*, trans. Willard Trask (New York, Harper & Row, 1958), p. 9.

sensibilities of another order that are now either being put aside or declining into atrophy. In the degree to which it deepens the sense of religious deprivation, a radically secular literature may, in other words, by a dialectical route bring us once again into proximity to the Presence that we had thought to be absent—and thus it may become itself a kind of witness to the Indestructible.

The late C. S. Lewis was on one occasion recalling the impact that George Macdonald's *Phantastes* had upon him, when he first chanced to read it in his youth: "It did nothing to my intellect nor (at that time) to my conscience. Their turn came far later and with the help of many other books and men. . . . What it actually did to me was to convert, even to baptize . . . my imagination."[37] Now it may be something like this —namely, a baptism of the imagination—that is deeply needed by every genuinely modern man, whether he recognizes it or not and whatever may be the creeds to which he formally gives his suffrage. To read the prayer with which the 90th Psalm begins—

Lord, thou hast been our dwelling-place in all generations.
Before the mountains were brought forth,
Or ever thou hadst formed the earth and the world,
Even from everlasting to everlasting, thou art God.

—to read such language as this is for all of us to know, however we may stand in regard to the things of religion, that here is a kind of capacity for naked encounter with the Sacred which few of us any longer possess. And what I am proposing is that, toward the end of a new baptism for the modern imagination, a radically secular literature may have a profoundly fruitful religious function to perform. For, by the very reso-

37. C. S. Lewis, *George Macdonald: An Anthology* (New York, Macmillan, 1947), p. 21. My attention has been called to this passage by my student, Gunnar Urang, who in a dissertation in progress at the University of Chicago, finds the fiction of C. S. Lewis, Charles Williams, and J. R. R. Tolkien to represent an attempt to "baptize" the modern imagination.

luteness with which it may plunge us into the Dark, it may precipitate us out of our forgetfulness, so that, in a way, our deprivation of the Transcendent may itself bring us into fresh proximity to its Mystery.

> They that wait upon the Lord shall renew their strength;
> they shall mount up with wings as eagles; they shall run and not be weary;
> they shall walk and not faint (Isaiah 40:31).

It is, I suspect, in some such circuitous and dialectical way as this that poetic experience in our time may become a *preparatio* for prayer.

KANSAS SCHOOL OF RELIGION
University of Kansas
1300 Oread Avenue
LAWRENCE, KANSAS 66044

Chapter Five CRITICISM
AND THEOLOGY—
THE TERMS OF THE ENGAGEMENT

Ours is a time in which, both life and thought being up against tremendous odds, we are all likely, in some degree or other, to be "crisis"-hunters, finding evidences of our general brokenness here, there, and everywhere. And, in my method of getting under way an estimate of the modern experiment in criticism, I do not myself propose to be an exception to the obsession of our age with *Tendenz*, since I suspect that any such estimate, from whatever point of view it may be undertaken, must begin by observing that criticism, too, is today in something like a situation of crisis. The crisis that I have in mind is one that arises out of what is central and decisive in the doctrines of modern poetics, and it was given a kind of desperate announcement a few years ago when Allen Tate bluntly raised the question which it is a peculiarity of our generation to be anxious about: "Is literary criticism possible?"[1]

It would not, of course, at first appear that the man of letters in our time feels himself to be at such an extremity, for one of the patron saints of the modern movement has assured us that the contemporary critic is "among the most presentable instances of modern man" and that in depth and precision his work is "beyond all earlier criticism in our language." On

1. The reference is to Mr. Tate's essay "Is Literary Criticism Possible? which appears in his book *The Forlorn Demon: Didactic and Critical Essays* (Chicago, Henry Regnery, 1953).

The Terms of the Engagement

all sides today we are frequently given similar testimonies of how unparalleled in any previous age are the vigor and trenchancy of criticism in our own time. Thus, with a zeal that is itself certainly unparalleled in any previous time, the contemporary movement is anthologized almost annually; and the editors of the journals in which it has gained expression frequently engage their colleagues in symposia the aim of which is to indicate the gains that have been made and the solid ground on which we may now take our stand. In all this stocktaking, however, I think we may sense a certain anxious uncertainty as to whether anything has been achieved at all and as to whether, in the presence of the great works of the past and of the modern period, we are yet able really to penetrate the ontological intransigence of the aesthetic fact. It is just possible that, despite the actual impressiveness of the achievement of modern criticism, this anxiety is a consequence of the doctrine which it has promoted and which has had the ironical effect of calling into question the very possibility of criticism itself. Indeed, what I want to propose is that, if we will reconsider the basic premises of modern poetics, we may be put in mind not only of what in part our present distresses in criticism derive from but also of the special kind of testimony about contemporary criticism that it may be necessary for a theorist to make whose fundamental bearings are of a theological sort.

When we seek the principal motives that underlie the general movement of criticism in our period, we cannot, of course, for long escape the recognition that, among them at least, has been the intention of many of its most distinguished representatives to offer some resistance to the reductionist tendency of modern scientism, particularly when it broaches upon those transactions with reality that are peculiar to the humanistic imagination. I can think of no single doctrine or emphasis that is subscribed to by all those writers who at one time or another have been held accountable for the New Criticism, but certainly by far the greater number of them are more of a single mind in their apprehensiveness about the reigning positivism than they are on any other single point. And it has been their unwillingness to give their suffrage to the absolute hegemony of empirical science which has decisively influenced their approach to the fundamental issues in theory of literature. Ours is a time in which it has been generally supposed that the only responsible versions of experience that can be had are those afforded us by the empirical sciences, and thus the common impulse has been to trivialize the arts by regarding them as merely a kind of harmless play which, at best, is to be tolerated for the sedative effect that it has on the nervous system. Even this assignment, however, hardly constitutes a satisfactory charter for the artist, since, in the ministry of health to the nervous system, he is not likely to compete successfully with our modern doctors of psychology. So, in the last analysis, our culture has been incapable of finding for the arts, and especially for literature, a valuable or an irreplaceable function. The result has been that the major strategists of modern criticism have felt it incumbent upon themselves to revindicate the poetic enterprise by doing what the culture was unable to do—by seeking to define that unique and indispensable role in the human economy that is played by imaginative literature and that can be preempted by nothing else.

This contemporary effort to specify the nature of the autonomy which a work of literary art possesses has involved a careful analysis of what is special in the linguistic strategies of the poet. The aim has been to establish that poetry is poetry and not another thing, for it has been recognized that in a culture so dominated by scientific procedure as is our own the common tendency is to hold all forms of discourse accountable to those critical canons that are really appropriate only to scientific modes of discourse—which, of course, then makes it possible for nonscientific modes of statement to be quickly dismissed on one pretext or another. Thus the tack that the contemporary movement in criticism has taken has been one that involves the denial that the poet is any sort of expositor at all. He is, we have been told, not an expositor, not a Platonist, not an allegorist, not a merchant in the business of ideas; on the contrary, he is a certain kind of technician, a certain kind of maker, who constructs out of language special sorts of things, such things as we call dramas and novels and poems. As the doctrine runs, what is distinctive about the language of imaginative literature is that, in contrast to the ordinary forms of discourse, it does not involve the reduction of words to the level of being merely conceptual signs. The mind is not led to appropriate the meaning of the individual components of a literary discourse by way of seeking those referents that are extrinsic to the discourse and to which its component terms presumably point. And our immunity from any compulsion to relate the language of the poem to an external reality has, in recent criticism, been understood in terms of the organic character of poetic structure. Which is to say that the contemporary critic has come to see poetic meaning not as a function of the relationships between the terms of the poem and some reality which is extrinsic to them, but rather as a function of the interrelationships that knit the terms together into the total pattern that forms the unity of the work. Our way of stating this distinctive character of poetic language is to say that its terms function not ostensively but reflexively, not semantically but syntactically—by which we mean that, unlike the situation that obtains in logical discourse in which the terms "retain their distinctive characters despite the relationship into which they have been brought,"[2] in poetic discourse they lose their distinctive characters, as they fuse into one another and are modified by what Cleanth Brooks calls "the pressure of the context."[3] It is, indeed, this whole phenomenon to which Mr. Brooks has appropriately applied the term irony, a concept that he has insisted upon in order to remark the radical extent to which the terms and "statements" of a literary work bear the pressure of the total context and have their meanings modified by that context. It

2. Ernest Cassirer, *Language and Myth*, trans. Susanne K. Langer (New York, Harper & Bros., 1946), p. 91.
3. Cleanth Brooks, "Irony as a Principle of Structure," in *Literary Opinion in America*, ed. Morton Dauwen Zabel (New York, Harper & Bros., 1951), pp. 730–31.

will be remembered that in a brilliant passage in *The Well Wrought Urn* he suggests that they ought even to be read as if they were speeches in a drama; since, as he says, if they are to be justified at all, it will not be by virtue of their "scientific or historical or philosophical truth, but [they will, rather, be] justified in terms of a principle analogous to that of dramatic propriety."[4]

It is in terms of this organic character of poetic structure that our generation has come to understand the resistance of literary art to the discursive paraphrase. It does not yield a series of paraphrasable abstractions because no set of terms of which a poetic work is constituted refers to anything extrinsic to the work; they refer, rather, to the other terms to which they are related within the work. Thus the perception of the meaning of the work awaits not an act of comparison between the component terms and the external objects or events which they may be taken to symbolize, but, rather, an act of imaginative prehension that will focus upon "the entire pattern of internal reference . . . apprehended as a unity."[5] The coherence of a work of imaginative literature is to be sought, in other words, not in any set of logically manageable propositions into which it may be paraphrased but rather in the living pattern of interrelated themes and "resolved stresses"[6] that the work contains.

There is, however, one inescapable fact that such a formulation of poetic meaning may at first appear to neglect, and it is the incorrigibly referential thrust that words do have. They like to function ostensively; which is to say, they insist on pointing to things. It makes no difference whether the things are actual or ideal; what counts is that they are extrinsic to

4. Cleanth Brooks, *The Well Wrought Urn* (London, Dennis Dobson, n.d.; originally pub. New York, Reynal and Hitchcock, 1947), p. 188.

5. Joseph Frank, "Spatial Form in Modern Literature," in *Criticism: The Foundations of Modern Literary Judgment,* ed. Mark Schorer, et al. (New York, Harcourt, Brace, 1948), p. 383. Mr. Frank's essay contains some very acute observations on the "reflexive" character of poetic language.

6. Brooks, *Well Wrought Urn,* p. 186.

the words themselves, for the words are not happy unless they are performing a semantic function. And, this being the case, it would seem that words would be intractable before the poetic purpose; but this problem is recognized by contemporary theorists who, indeed, have come to regard the poetic labor as involving in part an effort to deliver the word from its ordinary logical bonds and its inherent mediateness. As Ezra Pound once remarked, the poet

> takes words ordinarily having conventional objective meanings, and by forcing them into a new and independent structure objectifies fresh meanings. . . . The function of the artist is precisely the formulation of what has not found its way into language, i.e., any language, verbal, plastic or music.[7]

It is precisely this effort of the poet to perform not simply an act of denotation but the far more difficult act of evocation, of capturing and conveying the full, living body of the world and of objectifying fresh experience of it—it is this effort that very often commits him to the daring project of liberating words from the logical form into which they conventionally fall, so that they may be free to enter into the characteristic structures of poetic form in which they are affected by, and in turn affect, the total context established by the work. This is why you do not discover the meaning of a poem by taking an inventory of the various terms of which it is constituted and then by adding up the various meanings which these terms have in conventional usage. When contemporary criticism insists upon the foolishness of such a procedure, it does so because it is sensitive, perhaps above all else, to the marvelous violence of the action that is performed upon terms once they are drawn up into the poetic process, so that each alters under the aspect of the other and enters relationships that are completely irreducible to logical form. It is the mystery that T. S. Eliot had in mind when he remarked "that perpetual slight

7. Ezra Pound, "Epstein, Belgion and Meaning," *The Criterion,* 9, no. 36 (April 1930), p. 471.

alteration of language, words perpetually juxtaposed in new and sudden combination," which takes place in poetry.

We may say, then, by way of summary, that the redefinition in our time of the nature of literary art has led to the view that the given work exists in and through its language. What we have immediately before us is a patterned mosaic in language which is, in the phrase by which Denis de Rougemont speaks of the work of art in general, "a calculated trap for meditation"[8]—and as such it effectively insists that before it we perform an act of rapt and "intransitive attention."[9] One might even say that for the modern sensibility the poetry in the poem resides "not [in] some intrinsic quality (beauty or truth) of the materials"[10] with which the poet builds his poem, but rather in the completeness of the unity or composition that he contrives out of the stuff of language. What we begin with, as T. S. Eliot said, is simply "excellent words in excellent arrangement."[11]

This redefinition in modern criticism of "the mode of existence of a literary work of art" has in turn led to a redefinition of the creative process. So rigorous has been the stress laid on the autonomy of poetic language that language itself has often very nearly been regarded as the enabling cause of literary art. It is assumed that art is a virtue of the practical intellect and that the poet's vision is not fully formed until it has become objectified in language. Indeed, the executive principle of the creative process is considered really to derive not

8. Denis de Rougemont, "Religion and the Mission of the Artist," in *Spiritual Problems in Contemporary Literature*, ed. Stanley R. Hopper (New York, Harper & Bros., 1952), p. 177.

9. See Eliseo Vivas, "A Definition of the Esthetic Experience," in *The Problems of Aesthetics*, ed. Eliseo Vivas and Murray Krieger (New York, Rinehart, 1953), pp. 406–11. It is to Professor Vivas that we are indebted for the definition in contemporary aesthetics of the poetic experience in terms of "intransitive attention." This concept receives further elaboration in his book *Creation and Discovery*.

10. Cleanth Brooks, *Modern Poetry and the Tradition* (Chapel Hill, University of North Carolina Press, 1939), p. 43.

11. T. S. Eliot, Preface to the 1928 Edition, *The Sacred Wood*, 4th ed. (London, Faber and Faber, 1934), pp. ix–x.

The Terms of the Engagement

from the poet's metaphysic or his special perspective on the human story but rather from the medium to which his vision is submitted and by which it is controlled. It is regarded as a truism that whatever it is that the poet "says" about reality in a given work is something the content of which he himself did not fully possess until the completion of the work. As Murray Krieger has put it, "The poet's original idea for his work, no matter how clearly thought out and complete he thinks it is, undergoes such radical transformations as language goes creatively to work upon it that the finished poem, in its full internal relations, is far removed from what the author thought he had when he began."[12] The medium alone, in other words, objectifies the poet's materials and gives them their implications. This axiom of the contemporary movement in criticism was expressed with especial directness by R. P. Blackmur, when he remarked in his essay on Melville:

> Words, and their intimate arrangements, must be the ultimate as well as the immediate source of every effect in the written or spoken arts. Words bring meaning to birth and themselves contained the meaning as an imminent possibility before the pangs of junction. To the individual artist the use of words is an adventure in discovery; the imagination is heuristic among the words it manipulates. The reality you labour desperately or luckily to put into your words . . . you will actually have found there, deeply ready and innately formed to give an objective being and specific idiom to what you knew and did not know that you knew.[13]

Whatever it is, in other words, that is in the completed work is there by virtue of the language which controls the creative process and which produces the "new word" that the late Yvor Winters declared the authentic work of literary art to be. The poet does not have a version of the human situation

---

12. Murray Krieger, *The New Apologists for Poetry* (Minneapolis, University of Minnesota Press, 1956), p. 23.
13. R. P. Blackmur, "The Craft of Herman Melville: A Putative Statement," *The Lion and the Honeycomb*, p. 138.

to express, some imperious preoccupation to voice, or some difficult report to make; indeed, as Eliot proposed, there is no good reason for supposing that he does "any thinking on his own" at all, for it is not his business to think—not even poets as great as Dante and Shakespeare. All the writer need have is his medium, and, if he knows how to trust it and how to submit to it, it will do his work for him; it will, as Blackmur said, bring the "meaning to birth."

To be sure, what I have offered thus far is patently an abridgment of the advanced poetics of our time, but perhaps this account is at least sufficiently complex to provide some indication of the sources of the crisis that I earlier remarked as having arisen in contemporary criticism. It is clear certainly that many of the most distinguished theorists of our day have embraced a theory of literature which, when it falls into the hands of their epigones, can be so developed as to imply that the work of literary art is a linguistic artifact quite unattached to any independently existent reality. The fully achieved work of art, as the argument runs, is a discrete and closed system of mutually interrelated terms; the organic character of the structure prevents the constituent terms from being atomistically wrenched out of their context and made to perform a simple referential function, and it also succeeds in so segregating the total structure from the circumambient world as to prevent its entering into any extramural affiliation. "A poem should not mean but be," says Mr. MacLeish, and thereby, in this famous line from his poem "Ars Poetica," he summarizes, with a beautiful concision, the mind of a generation.

If, however, the work of literary art exists in complete isolation from all those contexts that lie beyond the one established by the work itself, if it neither points outward toward the world nor inward toward the poet's subjectivity, if it is wholly self-contained and cut off from the general world of meaning, why then it would seem that nothing really can be said about it at all. In this unpromising strait are we not all chargeable with "the heresy of paraphrase"? Mark Van Doren suggests in his book *The Noble Voice* that "Any great poet is in a sense beyond criticism for the simple reason that he has written a successful story," that "Criticism is most at home with failure," and that in the presence of the great success it must be "as dumb as the least instructed reader."[14] This is hardly an inspiriting conclusion for the practicing critic to reach; yet it is, in a way, the conclusion that has been enforced upon him by the new poetics of our period. The curious irony that has arisen out of the contemporary movement in criticism is a result of the fact that, on the one hand, it has striven for a concept of literary art that would permit responsible discussion of it as art rather than as something else; but, on the other hand, it has succeeded in so completely segregating art from everything else that, at least in principle, it has condemned itself to silence. And this is, I believe, the reason for the noticeable anxiety in the critical forum today about whether anything has really been achieved at all. Much has been achieved, of course, in the establishment of a fund of substantiated judgments about literary texts, but the point is that this achievement has had no great sanction in the body of principle to which our generation has often subscribed; for that body of doctrine has tended ultimately to represent the aesthetic fact as unavailable for critical discussion. Thus it should perhaps not be surprising that the same distinguished critic who some years ago told us that the contemporary achievement surpassed "all earlier criticism in our language" is also to be found wondering why it is that critics do not go mad; and one of his equally distinguished friends often ruminated (before his death a few years ago) on the "burden" that he and his colleagues in criticism must now bear.

The distresses and distempers that lead many of our most sensitive critics today to brood over the inhumanly difficult nature of their labors are, in other words, a result of their betrayal by the inadequate concept of literature that has descended from the main strategists of modern theory. There are many points at which this concept might now be put un-

14. Mark Van Doren, *The Noble Voice* (New York, Henry Holt, 1946), pp. 181–82.

der some pressure, but that on which I want chiefly to focus is the understanding of the creative process that has been promoted in our time, for here it is that we may get a good purchase on our present dilemmas. When this aspect of modern theory is examined, it becomes evident to how great a degree its legislation about the nature of the poetic object has determined its understanding of the process by which that object is made. What it has insisted upon is the indissoluble unity of form and content in the work which gives it the kind of autonomy that prevents its being translated into any other mode of statement. It is this concern which has led contemporary theorists to minimize the controlling effect upon the creative process of the writer's ideas and beliefs; for it has been supposed that, were any great tribute to be paid to these factors, we should be quickly on the way toward reinstating the heresy of didacticism, with its notion that the literary work is merely a rhetorical communication of independently formulable ideas.

Great stress, then, has been laid on the directive role of the medium in the creative process, and we have been reminded of how radical must be the transformations of the poet's ideas, once these ideas undergo the modifications necessitated by the exigencies of a developing linguistic structure. What we are asked to understand is that nothing really exists in imaginative literature, except as it is organized by the medium (which is language itself). Indeed, whatever does exist is itself created by the language, for, as I. A. Richards says, it is the "means of that growth which is the mind's endless endeavor to order itself."[15] Or, as the late R. P. Blackmur put it in the passage quoted earlier, "Words bring meaning to birth and themselves contained the meaning as an imminent possibility before the pangs of junction." The medium, in other words, is a kind of intelligent agency which in some mysterious way puppetizes the poet and does the job for which, in its innocence, common sense has traditionally held him responsible.

15. I. A. Richards, *The Philosophy of Rhetoric* (London and New York, Oxford University Press, 1936), p. 131.

The Terms of the Engagement

I am aware that at this point I am to some extent exaggerating the contemporary testimony, and my rough synopsis fails, happily, to render a fully adequate justice to the kind of extraordinarily brilliant and beautifully civilized discourse we are reading, say, in Cleanth Brooks's essay on *The Waste Land*, in Robert Penn Warren's essay on *The Ancient Mariner*, or in Allen Tate's essays on Dante and Poe. But the exaggerations in this matter of those hordes of their votaries who produce notes in "explication" for the academic quarterlies are, I think, often sufficiently great to make my characterization intelligible. In any event I am reassured by the coincidence between my own reaction and that of the English critic D. S. Savage, who suggested some years ago in the Preface to his book *The Withered Branch* that this "dizzy elevation" of the medium in contemporary criticism clearly leaves something important out of account.[16]

There is, I believe, no finer statement of what is unaccounted for than that which Jacques Maritain gives us in his great book *Creative Intuition in Art and Poetry*.[17] In this book, which grew out of his Mellon Lectures given during 1952 in the National Gallery in Washington, M. Maritain brought to a point of culmination forty years of study in the arts and in aesthetics. In one of its aspects the book has it as a major concern to call into question the modern notion that the creative process in art is merely an *operational* process and that the artist is merely a special sort of technician. "As to the great artists," he says, "who take pleasure in describing themselves as mere engineers in the manufacturing of an artifact of words or sounds, as Paul Valéry did, and as Stravinsky does, I think that they purposely do not tell the truth, at least completely. In reality the spiritual content of a creative intuition, with the poetic or melodic sense it conveys, animates their artifact, de-

16. D. S. Savage, *The Withered Branch* (New York, Pellegrini and Cudahy, n.d.), p. 12.
17. In the following account of this book that I give I have liberally raided two of the pages in an article of mine ("Maritain in His Role as Aesthetician") that appeared in *The Review of Metaphysics*, 8, no. 3 (March, 1955).

spite their grudge against inspiration."[18] This must be so, because, as M. Maritain insists, the activity which produces poetic art does not begin until the poet permits himself to be invaded by the reality of "things" and until he himself seeks to invade the deepest recesses of his own subjectivity—the two movements of the spirit being performed together, as though one, "in a moment of affective union." When the soul thus comes into profound spiritual contact with itself and when it also enters into the silent and mysterious depths of Being, it is brought back to "the single root" of its powers, "where the entire subjectivity is, as it were, gathered in a state of expectation and virtual creativity."[19] The whole experience becomes "a state of obscure . . . and sapid knowing."[20] Then,

> after the silent gathering a breath arises, coming not from the outside, but from the center of the soul—sometimes a breath which is almost imperceptible, but compelling and powerful, through which everything is given in easiness and happy expansion; sometimes a gale bursting all of a sudden, through which everything is given in violence and rapture; sometimes the gift of the beginning of a song; sometimes an outburst of unstoppable words.[21]

Only when this point in the artistic process has been reached may *operation* begin. For the artist to initiate the processes of operation at any earlier point is for him "to put the instrumental and secondary before the principal and primary, and to search for an escape through the discovery of a new external approach and new technical revolutions, instead of passing first through the creative source."[22] Then what is produced is but "a corpse of a work of art—a product of academicism."[23] "If creative intuition is lacking," he says, "a work can be perfectly made, and it is nothing; the artist has nothing

18. Jacques Maritain, *Creative Intuition in Art and Poetry*, p. 62.
19. Ibid., p. 239.
20. Ibid.
21. Ibid., p. 243.
22. Ibid., p. 223.
23. Ibid., p. 63.

to say. If creative intuition is present, and passes, to some extent, into the work, the work exists and speaks to us, even if it is imperfectly made and proceeds from a man who has the habit of art and a hand which shakes."[24]

At "the single root" of the poetic process, then, there is a profound act of creative intuition. And in this cognitive act, says M. Maritain, the soul "suffers things more than it learns them," experiencing them "through resonance in subjectivity." The thing that is cognitively grasped is simply "some complex of concrete and individual reality, seized in the violence of its sudden self-assertion and in the total unicity"[25] that is constituted by "all the other realities which echo in this existent, and which it conveys in the manner of a sign."[26] It is the richness of this imaginative prehension that gives life and power to the mathematic of poetic form.

M. Maritain is a good Thomist, and he does not therefore need to be reminded that art is "a virtue of the practical intellect" and that it requires "all the logic and shrewdness, self-restraint and self-possession of working intelligence."[27] Indeed, he insists upon the essential relation between art and reason, since it is reason that discovers the necessities in the nature of the medium that must be observed in order for the work to be brought into existence. But he also insists that the reason and the calculation that are in the poet "are there only to handle fire,"[28] and that to grant them anything more than this purely instrumental function, simply for the sake of adherence to a puritanical formalism and a spurious austerity, is to be guilty of a gratuitous dogmatism.

Many of us will doubtless find it difficult to accept M. Maritain's argument in this book in its entirety, for there are phases of his psychology—particularly those that bear upon his doctrine of the spiritual preconscious—that will surely

24. Ibid., p. 60.
25. Ibid., p. 126.
26. Ibid.
27. Ibid., p. 246.
28. Ibid., p. 218.

strike us as exceedingly cumbrous and perhaps even slightly obscurantist. I have adduced his testimony here not because it perfectly answers all of the questions that he raises; but, at a time when it is too much our habit to regard the medium as the single factor controlling the poetic process, M. Maritain's formulation of the problem has the very great merit of eloquently reminding us again of the actual primacy in the process of *poetic vision.* He discloses to us, that is, a stratagem for declaring once again that it is not language which brings meaning to birth and which enables the mind to order itself—not language, but *vision.*

Eliseo Vivas also helps us to some extent, I believe, with our difficulties when he reminds us that what is in part distinctive about the artist is his "passion for order."[29] "Really, universally," said Henry James, "relations stop nowhere, and the exquisite problem of the artist is eternally but to draw, by a geometry of his own, the circle within which they shall happily *appear* to do so."[30] That is to say, the artist wants to give a shape and a significance to what Mr. Vivas calls "the primary data of experience." He wants to contain the rich plenitude of experience within a pattern that will illumine and give meaning to its multifarious detail and its bewildering contingency. He cannot, of course, discover such a pattern unless he has a vantage point from which to view experience and by means of which his insights may be given order and proportion. Which is to say that he can transmute the viscous stuff of existential reality into the order of significant form only in accordance with what are his most fundamental beliefs about what is radically significant in life, and these beliefs he will have arrived at as a result of all the dealings that he has had with the religious, philosophical, moral, and social issues that the adventure of living has brought his way. The imaginative writer's beliefs, to be sure, are very rarely highly propositional in character; they do not generally involve a highly schema-

29. Vivas, *Creation and Discovery,* p. 117.
30. Henry James, *The Art of the Novel: Critical Prefaces* (New York, Charles Scribner's Sons, 1934), p. 5.

tized set of ideas or a fully integrated philosophic system. He customarily has something much less abstract, namely, a number of sharp and deeply felt insights into the meaning of the human story that control all his transactions with the world that lies before him. And it is by means of these insights that he discovers "the figure in the carpet."

The English novelist, Graham Greene, has said, "Every creative writer worth our consideration, every writer who can be called in the wide eighteenth-century use of the term a poet, is a victim: a man given to an obsession,"[31] or to what, in the eighteenth-century manner, Mr. Greene calls a "ruling passion." I take it that when he speaks in this way he has in mind the poet's habit of loyalty to some discovered method of construing experience, to some way of seeing things, by means of which he grapples and comes to terms with the tumultuous and fragmentary world that presses in upon him. Mr. Greene is alluding, in other words, to that act of consent which the poet gives to some fundamental hypothesis about the nature of existence—which itself in turn has the effect of ordering and making coherent the realities of immediate experience. And it is indeed, I believe, this act that constitutes the real beginning of the poetic process; the rest is largely a matter of the kind of knowledgeable experimentation within the limits of his medium that the expert craftsman engages in till he discovers what he wants to say gaining incarnation within a given form.

I am aware that I must appear to be advocating a view of the poetic process which, in point of fact, I do not hold at all. In much that I have just now said it may seem that I have been implying that, before even initiating the purely literary task, it is necessary for the poet to do an enormous amount of thinking. I have attributed to the writer's "metaphysic" or his "beliefs" a decisive role in the creative process, and thus it would seem that I believe it necessary for the writer to engage in a great deal of abstract thinking before that process can even be initiated. But this I do not think is true at all. I do not,

31. Graham Greene, *The Lost Childhood* (New York, Viking Press, 1952), p. 79.

of course, want to associate myself with that tendency in modern literary theory which supports the supposition that the writer is not a thinker at all. This is a notion which T. S. Eliot, I suppose, did more than anyone else to foster, and it is simply another instance of the confusion which his criticism, great as it is, occasionally contains. In his famous essay on "Shakespeare and the Stoicism of Seneca" he tells us, for example, that the poet does not "think" but that he makes poetry out of thought and that, therefore, he cannot as poet be said to "believe" in the system of thought that lies behind his poetry. In the particular case with which he is dealing, he tells us that Shakespeare did not really think; that he simply took the muddled and incompatible ideas of Seneca, Machiavelli, and Montaigne and made poetry out of them. And Eliot having— and properly so—the enormous prestige in our time that he has, it is not surprising that our generation should have become for a time so convinced that Shakespeare was not a profound thinker, if he was a thinker at all; that he merely assimilated and felicitously reexpressed well-worn truisms. Or, again, in the case of Dante, he tells us that Dante did not think either; that he simply took the magnificent formulations of St. Thomas and used them as the foundation of his poem. But surely there is great confusion here, for, as Fr. Martin Jarrett-Kerr has remarked, "If . . . we start from the initial conviction that one of the first marks of the major poet or novelist is the possession of a *fine mind*, we must refuse to concede that Shakespeare or Dante did not think but had their thinking done for them."[32]

Eliot's error here resulted, I suspect, from the supposition that to acknowledge the poet as a thinker is in effect to say that the poetic process originates in a highly developed system of ideas, and this is, of course, not at all the case. What I have been calling the writer's beliefs are rarely if ever the highly propositional things that Eliot, in denying them the importance which I have given them, seemed to think they are. For

---

32. Martin Jarrett-Kerr, C. R., *Studies in Literature and Belief* (New York, Harper & Bros., 1955), p. 5.

what the writer generally has is not a system of belief but rather *an imagination* of what is radically significant.

In insisting upon the writer's necessary dependence upon his beliefs, I am not intending, then, to suggest that the poet or the novelist must, first of all, be a philosopher or a theologian—though, on the other hand, I am not in accord with Eliot's contention that the poet is not really a thinker at all, a contention which is significantly contradicted by Eliot's own career in poetry. There is a distinction somewhere in St. Thomas which illumines, I think, the nature of the poet's relation to his beliefs. St. Thomas distinguishes between *cognitio per modum cognitionis*—knowledge, that is, in the manner of or by means of the intelligence or the discursive reason—and *cognitio per modum inclinationis*—knowledge, that is, in the manner of or by means of inclination. And what I would suggest is that the poet holds his "first principles" or his beliefs or his metaphysic *per modum inclinationis*—that is, inclinatorily. Which is to say that his beliefs point in the direction of a coherent philosophy of life toward which his sensibility has an irresistible inclination and in which it finds its necessary sanction. The contrast between the two modes of cognition is, to be sure, not an absolute contrast, and what it is therefore proper to say is that it is the *tendency* of the poet to hold his beliefs *per modum inclinationis;* though there are some writers, Eliot among them, who also hold their beliefs *per modum cognitionis*. But in whatever manner they may be held in the individual case, what I am now insisting upon principally is the precedence and the primacy of the act by which the poet searches experience and finds therein an ultimate concern that gives him then a perspective upon the flux and the flow.

Whatever it is, of course, that concerns the poet ultimately, that constitutes his "ruling passion" and the substance of his vision, is something to which the critic can be attentive only as it is discoverable in the work. By now surely we have all taken to heart the lesson of Messrs. Wimsatt and Beardsley on the International Fallacy, and we understand the irrelevance of any essay in literary criticism that is based on some process of armchair psychoanalysis which seeks to elevate the biographical category of the artist's conscious intention into a category of aesthetic discrimination.[33] But the designation of "intentionalism" as fallacious becomes itself a fallacy if it is made to support the view that a work of literary art is "a merely formal structure devoid of embodied meanings and values."[34] For such aesthetic objects, though "they may be found in the realm of pure design or pure music,"[35] simply do not exist in the realm of literature where surely a main part of the critic's task involves the discovery of "the actual operative intention which, as telic cause, accounts for the finished work"[36] and which can be defined only in terms of the vision of the world which it serves.

The authentic work of literary art, says M. de Rougemont, is a trap for the attention, but he also says that it is an "oriented trap." It is a trap, in the sense that, having the kind of autonomy that modern criticism has claimed for it, it "has for its specific function . . . the magnetizing of the sensibility, the fascinating of the meditation";[37] as Mr. Vivas would put it, it can command upon itself an act of "intransitive attention." But the trap is oriented; it focuses the attention, that is, upon something which transcends the verbal structure itself, this simply being the circumambient world of human experience, in those of its aspects that have claimed the poet's concern. Thus it is that the autonomy of the work is no more an absolute thing than is the intransitivity of the reader's attention, for both are qualified by the implicative relations that branch out indefinitely from the aesthetic fact toward the world by which that fact is surrounded.

Here it is, then, that we may discover the point of entry into the literary work that we have. For it is analysis of the sort

33. W. K. Wimsatt and Monroe Beardsley, "The Intentional Fallacy," *The Sewanee Review*, 54 (Summer 1946), pp. 468–88.
34. Vivas, *Creation and Discovery*, p. 172.
35. Ibid.
36. Ibid., p. 164.
37. De Rougemont, "Religion and the Mission of the Artist," p. 176.

that we have been conducting that reveals that the work is not a closed system and that it does not have that quality of "aseity" which Scholastic theologians have considered the godhead to possess, by reason of the self-derived and eternally independent character of its being. The work is not wholly self-contained and utterly cut off from the reader, because, in the creative process, the aesthetic intentions of the artist are not segregated from all that most vitally concerns him as a human being but are, on the contrary, formed by these concerns and are thus empowered to orient the work toward the common human experience. This experience has, of course, to be grasped in and through the structures by means of which it is aesthetically rendered. But to stress the fact that poetic art signifies by means of its structure need not, I think commit us to a formalism so purist as to require the view that the autonomy of the work is absolute. As I have been insisting, great literature does, in point of fact, always open outward toward the world, and that which keeps the universe of poetry from being hermetically sealed off from the universe of man is the poet's vision that it incarnates, of spaces and horizons, of cities and men, of time and eternity. Thus no truly civilized account of *Mansfield Park* or *The Portrait of a Lady* or *The Good Soldier* will be merely an affair of compiling a series of notations on how page 68 anticipates page 173 and how both are somehow knotted together by page 213, or on how stanza v "ironically qualifies" stanza iii and how the images of circularity in stanza vi are modified and balanced off by the images of linearity in stanza vii. For all of the attractiveness which this kind of gibberish has somehow come to have for many of the bright young men who teach literature in our universities today, it is a sort of slang which the truly great critics of our period (Leavis, Brooks, Tate, Trilling) have never adopted. The poem in itself, in other words, as merely a structure of language, is simply a naked abstraction, for the real poem, the real novel, is something that we begin to appropriate only as we seek some knowledge of the context of belief and the quality of vision out of which it springs and with reference to which the words on the printed page have their fullest and richest meaning.

We have, I think, now arrived at the point in our argument at which it is finally possible for me to say that the aspect of poetic art to which I have been referring by the terms *vision* and *belief* is precisely the element which we ought to regard as constituting the religious dimension of imaginative literature. When I speak of the religious dimension of literary art, in other words, I do not have in mind any special iconic materials stemming from a tradition of orthodoxy which may or may not appear in a given work. Were it to be so conceived, it might indeed then be something peripheral and inorganic to the nature of literature itself; whereas the way of regarding our problem that I now want to recommend is one that involves the proposal that the religious dimension is something intrinsic to and constitutive of the nature of literature as such. I am here guided in my understanding of what is religious in the orders of cultural expression by the conception of the matter that was so ably advanced by the late Paul Tillich. In all the work that he did in the philosophy of culture over more than forty years, the persistent strain that is to be noted is one arising out of his insistence upon what might be called the coinherence of religion and culture. He liked to say that "Religion is the substance of culture and culture the form of religion."[38] He remarked, for example,

> If any one, being impressed by the mosaics of Ravenna or the ceiling paintings of the Sistine Chapel, or by the portraits of the older Rembrandt, should be asked whether his experience was religious or cultural, he would find the answer difficult. Perhaps it would be correct to say that his experience was cultural as to form, and religious as to substance. It is cultural because it is not attached to a specific ritual-activity; and religious, because it evokes questioning as to the Absolute or the limits of human existence. This is

38. Paul Tillich, *The Protestant Era* (Chicago, University of Chicago Press, 1948), p. 57.

equally true of painting, of music and poetry, of philosophy and science. . . . Wherever human existence in thought or action becomes a subject of doubts and questions, wherever unconditioned meaning becomes visible in works which only have conditioned meaning in themselves, there culture is religious.[39]

Dr. Tillich acknowledged that it was indeed to the theoretical comprehension of this "mutual immanence of religion and culture" that his philosophy of religion was primarily dedicated. "No cultural creation," he said, "can hide its religious ground,"[40] and its religious ground is formed by the "ultimate concern" to which it bears witness; for that, as he insisted, is what religion is: it "is ultimate concern."[41] And since it is religion, in this sense, that is truly substantive in the various symbolic expressions of a culture, the task of criticism, in whatever medium it may be conducted, is, at bottom, that of deciphering the given work at hand in such a way as to reveal the ultimate concern which it implies. As he said, in the depth of every cultural creation "there is an ultimate . . . and [an] all-determining concern, something absolutely serious,"[42] even if it is expressed in what are conventionally regarded as secular terms.

It should, of course, be said that, in these definitions, Paul Tillich was not seeking to identify religion and culture; but he did want to avoid the error that T. S. Eliot cautioned us against "of regarding religion and culture as two separate things between which there is a relation."[43] What he recognized was that the whole cultural process by which man expresses and realizes his rational humanity is actually governed by what are his most ultimate concerns—his concerns, that is,

39. Paul Tillich, *The Interpretation of History* (New York, Charles Scribner's Sons, 1936), p. 49.
40. Tillich, *The Protestant Era*, p. 57.
41. Ibid., p. 59.
42. Ibid., pp. 58–59.
43. T. S. Eliot, *Notes Towards the Definition of Culture* (New York, Harcourt, Brace, 1949), pp. 31–32.

"with the meaning of life and with all the forces that threaten or support that meaning."[44] And, in passing, it is, I think, worth remarking that it was this profoundly realistic approach to the problem of cultural interpretation that enabled Dr. Tillich to see that in our own period the most radically religious movements in literature and painting and music may gain expression in strangely uncanonical terms—sometimes even in despairing maledictions and in apocalyptic visions of the abyss of disintegration that threatens the world today. As he often wanted to say, in the very profundity with which *Wozzeck* and the *Guernica* and *The Waste Land* express the disorder of the times there is an equally profound witness to the spiritual order that has been lost, so that these great expressions of the modern movement in art are rather like an uncertain prayer that corresponds to the second petition of the *Our Father*.[45]

We are now, then, brought to the point at which we must regather our bearings by a final act of recapitulation. We have said that the work of literary art is a special sort of linguistic structure that traps the attention intransitively; but we have also argued that the intransitivity of the reader's attention is not absolute, since the autonomy of the object which captures his attention is not itself absolute. The literary work is a trap, but it is a trap that is oriented toward the world of existence that transcends the work—and the work is oriented by the vision, by the belief, by the ultimate concern of which it is an incarnation: its orientation, that is to say, is essentially religious. And this is why criticism itself must, in the end, be theological. The prevailing orthodoxy in contemporary criticism, to be sure, generally represents hostility toward the idea of metaphysical and theological considerations being

44. James Luther Adams, "Tillich's Concept of the Protestant Era," Editor's Appendix, *The Protestant Era*, p. 273.

45. M. de Rougemont says that "art would appear to be like an invocation (more often than not unconscious) to the lost harmony, like a prayer (more often than not confused), corresponding to the second petition of the Lord's Prayer—'Thy Kingdom come.'" See "Religion and the Mission of the Artist," p. 186.

introduced into the order of critical discourse. But, as Leslie
Fiedler has remarked,

> The "pure" literary critic, who pretends, in the cant phrase,
> to stay "inside" a work all of whose metaphors and mean-
> ings are pressing outward, is only half-aware. And half-
> aware, he deceives; for he cannot help smuggling unexam-
> ined moral and metaphysical judgments into his "close
> analyses," any more than the "pure" literary historian can
> help bootlegging unconfessed aesthetic estimates into his
> chronicles. Literary criticism is always becoming "some-
> thing else," for the simple reason that literature is always
> "something else."[46]

Our abdication from the reigning poetics of our time is,
however, only partial, for the religious dimension of literature, as we have defined it, must be regarded as something
which, in so far as it is really a datum for critical inspection
and assessment, exists in the language of the work. The only
thing that lies before the critic is a composition in language,
and it is, presumably, his skill in the supervision of language
that primarily distinguishes the literary artist; surely it would
be wrongheaded to assume that the thing that makes him an
artist is the profundity or the novelty of his vision. On the
contrary, he makes good his vocational claim in the republic
of letters by the extent of the success with which he shapes
the substance of experience, in accordance with his vision of
what it is that makes it ultimately meaningful. And he can
give a significant form or shape to experience only in so far as
he takes the highest kind of advantage of the medium in
which his art is wrought.

So it may then, I think, be taken for granted that whatever
it is that orients a work of literary art or that constitutes the
ultimate concern that it embodies is something that will disclose itself in the ways in which the writer brings the resources
of language into the service of his project. Thus we shall want

46. Leslie Fiedler, "Toward an Amateur Criticism," *The Kenyon Review*, 12, no. 4 (Autumn 1950), p. 564.

very carefully to preserve all that has been gained in modern criticism as a result of its researches into the problem of how the language of imaginative literature is to be understood and talked about. For the critic, however, to insist upon remaining merely a kind of grammarian is for him to forego many of the most interesting and significant discriminations that literary criticism can make. Though the literary work is a special sort of linguistic structure, that which holds the highest interest for us is the special seizure of reality which this structure is instrumental toward. It is, in other words, the nature of literature itself that compels the critic finally to move beyond the level of verbal analysis to the level of metaphysical and theological valuation. On this level, of course, he can establish the propriety of his judgments only by reference to his own insight, his own scale of values, his own sense of what is important in art and in life. As the English critic, the late S. L. Bethell, remarked,

> if he is a Christian worthy of the name, his whole outlook will be coloured by his religion; he will see life in Christian terms, and, though he may ignore an atheist writer's professed atheism, he will still judge his degree of insight into character by his own insight, which will have been formed in part by his Christian experience. And the non-Christian critic—let us be clear about this—will also judge a writer's insight into character (or into anything else, of course) by the standard of his own insight, however derived. There is no "impartial criticism" in this sense, or rather there is no critical neutrality; there are only Christian critics and Marxist critics and Moslem critics—and critics who think themselves disinterested but who are really swayed unconciously by the beliefs they have necessarily acquired by being members of a particular society in a particular place and time.[47]

47. S. L. Bethell, *Essays on Literary Criticism and the English Tradition* (London, Dennis Dobson, 1948), pp. 24–25.

The Terms of the Engagement

And, as Bethell observed with great shrewdness,

> the last are really the least impartial, for, believing them-
> selves impartial, they are open to every unconscious influ-
> ence upon their judgment, while the "doctrinaire" critic
> may keep his doctrine well in view and, if not entirely avoid-
> ing prejudice, may at least give his readers fair warning of
> what to expect.[48]

At this point the question may well be raised as to whether
my use of these quotations from Bethell is calculated to suggest that we are justified in trying to guarantee literary art by
the quality of belief that it possesses. And, were this question
to be put to me, my impulse, as a Christian, would, I think, be
to say, with Professor Roy W. Battenhouse, that "the good
poet should be able, like Adam in the Garden, to name every
creature correctly. Apprehending the form of each thing that
is brought before him, he should be able to assign it its proper
place."[49] But, of course, this capacity, which so influentially
determines the outcome of the artistic process, is itself very
largely dependent upon the artist's metaphysical or religious
orientation—so that, as a Christian, I should again feel
prompted to say, with Mr. Battenhouse, that,

> if it is true that the light with which an artist sees inclines
> to affect the justness of his observations, the presence of
> full light cannot but clarify the issues of proportion and
> order. With inadequate lighting, the artist will not see cer-
> tain things he ought to see; it will be all too easy for him to
> draw disproportionately what he does see. To put it another
> way the artist who takes up his location in Plato's cave has
> not the same chance as he who sets up shop by Christ's
> open tomb.[50]

48. Ibid., p. 25.
49. Roy W. Battenhouse, "The Relation of Theology to Literary Criticism," *The Journal of Bible and Religion*, *13*, no. 1 (February 1945), p.
20.
50. Ibid.

In principle, I should, in other words, expect the Christian reader at least—all other things being equal—more enthusiastically to give his suffrage to a literature that was Christianly oriented than to one which was not. But now, not as a matter of principle but as a matter of fact, the Christian reader lives in a period whose characteristic quality, at least ever since the Renaissance, has been defined, as Erich Heller has reminded us, not merely by a dissociation of faith from knowledge but by what has been the more profound severance of faith from sensibility. "It is this rift," says Professor Heller, "which has made it impossible for most Christians not to *feel*, or at least not to feel *also* as true many 'truths' which are incompatible with the truth of their faith."[51] They have, in other words, been in something like the position of the father of the possessed child whom the Synoptist records as having cried out, "Lord, I believe; help thou mine unbelief" (Mark 9:24). And, this being the case, the Christian reader will actually respond to the various constructions of the human story that he encounters in literature with a latitudinarianism that will, at least in part, be akin to that which any other sensitive reader in our time brings to bear upon his dealings with literary art. That is to say, what he will require is that the view of life that is conveyed by the given poem or novel commend itself as a possible view, as one to which an intelligent and sensitive observer of the human scene might be led by a sober consideration of the facts of experience. Though he will agree with Eliot that to judge a work of art by artistic standards and to judge it by religious standards ought perhaps to "come in the end to the same thing,"[52] he will recognize, as Eliot did, that, in our time, this is an end at which most of us will have great difficulty in arriving.

But, hesitant as the Christian critic ought to be in defining for himself a program whose rigor would have the effect of delimiting the range of his sympathies and of isolating him from the actualities of the literary life, we may yet, I think,

51. Erich Heller, *The Disinherited Mind*, p. 125.
52. Eliot, *Notes*, p. 29.

put to him the question as to what in general will be his special approach to the literature of our own period. Here we must remember, as Amos Wilder has so well said, that "the most significant art of the twentieth century—Stravinsky, Picasso, Joyce, Kafka, Pound, Eliot—is that which comes immediately out of the epochal convulsions of the time, out of full immersion in the condition of man today."[53] And, since this is so, we should not be surprised that "the fountains of spiritual renewal" in literature, as Dr. Wilder says, have often broken forth "outside the churches in uncanonical witness, prayer and celebration."[54]

The crypto-religious character of many of the basic impulses in modern literature has, of course, often been remarked, and we must remain mindful that the artist's failure to canalize these impulses in the direction of explicit Christian affirmation is, very frequently, not to be ascribed simply to his intransigent agnosticism, but, rather, to the Christian community's failure to present itself to him as something with which he might really make common cause. This is why "the protagonists of traditional values, the witnesses of the older covenants and charters of our common life, the saints in the sense of the dedicated and disciplined individuals who assume the costs of nonconformity, the martyrs or scapegoats of the general crisis"—this is why all these are often "found in secular guise, unordained except by the authenticity of their utterance."[55] And the recognition of these ambivalences and dislocations by the Christian critic must be the starting point, I believe, of any transaction into which he may enter with the world of modern art.

The great effort of the Christian critic in our day should no doubt have as its ultimate aim a reconciliation between the modern arts and the Church, between the creative imagination and the Christian faith. But the immense obstacles on the side of art and on the side of the Church that hinder this

53. Amos N. Wilder, *Modern Poetry*, p. 176.
54. Ibid., p. 268.
55. Ibid.

achievement are not to be minimized. The great misfortune is that those modern writers who have experienced most profoundly the intellectual and spiritual predicaments of the time and whose embrace of a Christian position would therefore be most arresting are often those who are most acutely sensible of the failure of institutional Christianity—especially of Protestantism—to give due place to "the yea-saying impulse of the biblical faith and its moment of creative play."[56] It is felt "that a Christian so sterilizes his heart that there is no concern left for art and the rich play, the riot and fecundity of life."[57] It is the rejection of a Christianity that is felt to be ascetical and world-denying which forms the rule among modern writers rather than the exception: Yeats, Joyce, Wallace Stevens, and many others have refused the Gospel, very largely, one feels, because of the failure of its interpreters to express what Amos Wilder feels to be the genuine element of antinomianism in the Gospel itself.[58] He puts the issue with great clarity in his book *The Spiritual Aspects of the New Poetry:*

> For the poets the scandal of Christ is his asceticism. The very medium of their art as poets; indeed, the very element of their experience as men, is the gamut of human living, emotions, drama. "Man's resinous heart" and the loves, loyalties, the pride, the grief it feeds—these are the stuff of poetry and the sense of life. And the Cross lays its shadow on this; it draws away all the blood from the glowing body of existence and leaves it mutilated and charred in the hope of some thin ethereal felicity. The wine of life is changed to water. . . . The "dramatic caves" of the human heart and imagination are renounced for some wan empyrean of spiritual revery. The very word "spiritual" has come to signify inanity and vacuity. The refusal of religion by the modern

56. Ibid., p. 243.
57. Amos N. Wilder, *The Spiritual Aspects of the New Poetry* (New York, Harper & Bros., 1940), pp. 197–98.
58. See Wilder, *Modern Poetry*, chap. 10.

poet, and by more than moderns and by more than poets, goes back to the apparent denial of human living by religion, to the supposed incompatibility of life with Life and of art with faith.[59]

That this is the major hindrance on the side of art to a reconciliation between the creative imagination and the Church one may very quickly discover by a perusal of what is still one of the most interesting spiritual documents of our period, the *Partisan Review* symposium, *Religion and the Intellectuals* (1950), in which the general testimony of many of the most influential literary figures of our day tends to confirm Professor Wilder's assessment.

There are also serious hindrances on the side of the Church to a rapprochement between art and faith. There are many religious people who suppose their own conservative and unaroused attitudes toward modern life to be based on valid Christian principles, when they really derive from a protected social situation in which it has been possible for them to shut their eyes to the dislocations of the age to which history has committed us all. They face with defensiveness and hostility much of modern literature in which these stresses and strains are reflected, and they insist upon the excessiveness of its alarmism and its irrelevance to the world in which they choose to believe that they live. It is their habit to speak of many of the major writers of this century—Pound and Gide, Joyce and Lawrence, Kafka and Faulkner—as if the difficulties presented by their work were merely frivolous and as if the inclination of their vision toward a tragic perspective were a consequence merely of psychological eccentricity. And they mistake their censoriousness with respect to the modern artist for a genuinely Christian position. A more sophisticated version of the same unfriendliness to the modern arts arises out of the extreme disjunctions between the natural order and the order of revelation that are insisted upon in those currents of Protestant thought stemming from Crisis-theology. In this theological

59. Wilder, *Spiritual Aspects*, p. 196.

framework the arts, as a department of human culture, are comprehended in terms of their issuance from the natural order, all of whose fruits are, of course, to be viewed, as a matter of principle, with a deep suspicion and scepticism. The difficulties, in other words, that hinder reconciliation in our day between the modern artist and the Church seem to be, as Wladimir Weidlé suggested many years ago in his penetrating book *The Dilemma of the Arts*, difficulties of "mutual incomprehension."[60]

One thing, however, is, I believe, fairly certain, and that is that the Christian community will not succeed in relating itself creatively to the modern artist if it attempts to do so by laying down its law, by hedging him about with rules and programs demanding his prompt obedience. Its proper course is perhaps most clearly set forth in a set of distinctions that Paul Tillich made central to his philosophy of culture. Those who are familiar with his thought will recall that there were three terms for which he had a great liking. He often spoke of "autonomy," of "heteronomy," and of "theonomy," and we need carefully to keep in mind what is at issue in the distinctions that he drew between these terms. In each case, it will be noticed, the suffix derives from the Greek *nomos*, meaning usage or the law of human life; so the three terms stand for different versions of what the nature of that law is.

The prefix of the first, autonomy, derives from the Greek *autos*, meaning "self"; and thus the term points to that view of the law of life which suggests that man is himself the source of it and that the culture which he creates is not therefore to be measured by reference to any ultimate principle transcendent to the rational and the human. The prefix of the second term, heteronomy, derives from the Greek *heteros*, meaning "that which is other than, different from, alien to, strange"; so, when Tillich used this term, he had in mind those ecclesiastical and political communities that relate themselves to the enterprises of culture by hedging them about with laws

60. Wladimir Weidlé, *The Dilemma of the Arts*, trans. Martin Jarrett-Kerr, C. R. (London: S. C. M. Press, 1948), chap. 6.

and authoritative criteria that are not organic to their nature. Finally, the prefix of the third term has its origin in the Greek word *theos*, meaning "god," and Tillich employed the concept of theonomy to designate that view of culture which understands the divine law to be "at the same time, the innermost law of man himself,"[61] which regards the transcendent as being not a dimension external to, and therefore to be imposed upon, man's cultural life but rather as the inescapable spiritual ground of all our art and philosophy and science. Autonomy, in other words, represents the attempt to cut the ties of a culture with its transcendent ground, with anything ultimate and unconditional; heteronomy represents "the attempt of a religion to dominate autonomous cultural creativity from the outside,"[62] while a theonomy is "a culture in which the ultimate meaning of existence shines through all finite forms of thought and action; the culture is transparent, and its creations are vessels of a spiritual content."[63]

Dr. Tillich's contention was that the way of heteronomy can never be the way of a truly radical Christianity. The Church's method of addressing culture must, to be sure, involve a criticism of "self-complacent autonomy," but always, he insisted, the Christian community, when it is alive to the full implications of an Incarnational faith, will remember that "in the depth of every autonomous culture an ultimate concern, something unconditional and holy, is implied." And the genius of authentically Christian humanism is most truly expressed when, in its dealings with what is called "secular culture," it so takes this body of witness up into itself that the distinction between the sacred and the secular ceases to exist.

It will, I believe, be along this way—the way of "theonomy" —that a reunion of art and religion, if it is to occur at all, will be achieved. But, of course, what will be chiefly required is an infinite degree of tact and humility in the Christian critic, and

61. Tillich, *The Protestant Era*, pp. 56–57.
62. Ibid., p. xvi.
63. Ibid.

143

Criticism and Theology—

thus a reconciliation between art and faith in our day would be, as Wladimir Weidlé has reminded us,

the symptom of a renewal of the religious life itself. When frozen faith melts again, when it is once more love and freedom, then will be the time that art will light up again at the new kindling of the fire of the spirit. There seem to be many indications that such a future is possible; and in any case it is the only future still open to art. There is one way alone—and there is no other—because artistic experience is, deep down, a religious experience, because the world art lives in cannot be made habitable save by religion alone.[64]

64. Weidlé, *Dilemma*, p. 125.

144

Chapter Six

ON THE PLACE OF
             LITTERAE HUMANIORES
IN THE CURRICULUM
OF THEOLOGICAL STUDIES

It begins to be widely noticed that the most significant recent innovation in the teaching of theology on the American scene has entailed the initiating, within the context of the theological curriculum itself, of studies in Humane Letters, most especially in the literature of the modern period. It will doubtless seem a little odd to some that university faculties of theology should be making provision in their curricula, as they increasingly are, for the systematic study of the various forms of imaginative literature. A visitor from some other department of academic life entering a hall of divinity may naturally be expected to imagine that here are to be found scholars at work on the canonical texts of the Church, on the many complicated strands of the history of the Church, and on the rich and various tradition of its theological formulations. Indeed such a visitor might perhaps be prepared to expect that, in a divinity faculty whose orientation is basically Christian, it would also be felt to be important to pay a large amount of attention to the phenomenology of the religious impulse in its various great expressions outside the world of Christendom. But he may no doubt be entitled to a certain astonishment, when he finds not only these and other related enterprises under way but finds also theologians who are seriously handling the materials of drama and fiction and poetry—and not merely, or even principally, in those special phases where formally Christian motifs are present in an explicit way. And this visitor, if he brings some antecedent scepticism about the validity of any enfranchisement at all for theological pursuits in the university, may even suspect that, in a theological faculty, a department of study in which a Rimbaud or a Brecht or a Faulkner is at the fore does itself simply attest perhaps to a basic insecurity by which the total enterprise of theology is (quite properly) infected in our time.

In 1961 Professor Ernest Sirluck of the University of Toronto (then, of the University of Chicago), in a review published in *Modern Philology*, turned his splendid gift for polemic on the not very invulnerable target presented by a book that had appeared in the previous year, on Milton and Bunyan—"and," as its title stated, "the Great Theologians." Though written by a professional scholar, it is a book without any real urbanity of scholarship or grace of style, and Professor Sirluck could therefore, and did, swiftly expose its general unsatisfactoriness (most especially in the simplistic account that is given of Milton's religious position). For all of what he found, however, to be stale and gauche in this essay, the book yet struck him as having a certain lively interest, in the degree to which it stood for him as an expression of "the New Apologetic"—whereby the contemporary Christian apologist (for what Professor Sirluck's tone leads one to feel is in his view an essentially bankrupt tradition) attempts to shore up a crumbling edifice by attaching it to prestigious cultural forms—whose "attitudes, insights, presuppositions, and principles [he analyses] and relates . . . to, corrects . . . by, and reinforces . . . with religion. . . . From the human work, thus enhanced, he then deduces validation for the religion, or some aspect of the religion, he teaches." Thus it is, says Professor Sirluck, that the New Apologetic proceeds, "aided by the multiplication of eleemosynary foundations for the support of religion in higher education, religion in art, religion in literature, etc., and by the consequent proliferation of university and seminary programs and courses built upon this interest."

It is such a response as this that can most assuredly be expected from certain quarters, when the actuality of the curriculum in the major centers of American theological education is discovered to be the complex interdisciplinary undertaking that it has come to be. For what the visitor from some other department of the academic community will find there is not only a vigorous enterprise of research and teaching in the traditional areas of biblical study, theology, and church history but also a lively enterprise of research into the various modes of the mutual involvement between Christian tradition and the general fabric of culture. He will find, for example, strict attention being paid to traditional and to modern philosophy; he will discover that, on the contemporary scene, a Wittgenstein or a Merleau-Ponty is being studied as rigorously as a Barth or a Rahner. It will be apparent that the most careful stock is being taken of the sciences of man, both social and psychological, that Weber and Lévi-Strauss, that Freud and Erikson are being scanned as closely as are Bultmann and Tillich. And the full gamut of the intellectual situation with which Christianity today finds itself engaged will be seen to claim a very large place in the forum of a university faculty of theology.

It was a social scientist, the historian Donald Meyer, who noticed a few years ago with a good deal of surprise how carefully the theological community today is often to be found addressing itself to the literary imagination and to the whole spectrum of the arts. Toward the close of a book devoted to an analysis of political thought in American Protestantism since the War of 1918,[1] Professor Meyer remarks the extent to which, starting already in the early 1950s, the great themes of the artistic culture of our period begin to compete with the issues of politics for the attention of American theology. And here, too, is an area of man's self-interpretation that has been felt often to be raising, as it were, essentially theological questions about human existence, and with such a brilliance and power as invited the most considered kind of response from those whose business it is formally to articulate and in-

1. See Donald B. Meyer, *The Protestant Search for Political Realism* (Berkeley and Los Angeles, University of California Press, 1960).

terpret the Christian sense of reality. So the inquiry of academic theology into the total transaction to be negotiated between Christianity and its present cultural environment has increasingly borne in upon the aesthetic realm, and large place has been given in the major theological faculties to this whole field of problems, most especially as it involves the literary imagination and its rendering of modern experience.

Now it is an interesting fact of our cultural life that those for whom the issues of religion are of no real importance at all can be counted on to have the strictest notions as to what religion ought to be and do. Their preference seems normally to be for a religion that is anti-intellectualist and hostile to cultural enterprise; and, when its appeal is to some form of the *credo quia absurdum,* they can then comfortably utter the conventional expressions of bemusement and dismay at the terrible *sacrificium intellectus* which it exacts. When, on the other hand, they confront a religion which is affirmative of the vitalities of culture and which looks toward some sort of reciprocity between itself and those vitalities, they indignantly declare it to be a fraud; tears are shed over its misguidedly emptying itself of its own native substance and uniqueness; and there is much condescending talk about some New Apologetic which, it is implied, simply betokens a loss of self-confidence and the consequent desire on the part of the strategists of religious thought to become fellow travelers of whatever is modish and *au courant,* in the hope that their position may thereby win some slight strengthening.

In point of fact, however, the kind of close attention which is given to the modern cultural scene in the great centers of theological education in this country today—at Yale, Chicago, Harvard, Union Seminary—is not at all prompted by any frivolous fascination with what is approved and *recherché.* It stems rather from a profound reconstitution in Christian theology of its own self-understanding—which in our time follows upon a very radical repossession of the biblical message and, consequently, a drastically changed conception of the cultural stance to which the Christian enterprise is committed by that message.

Here, the decisive development—prepared for by a long line of distinguished modern research into the mentality of the biblical people—is the discovery, gradually shaping over the past thirty years, that the sovereign intention of biblical faith (and hence of Christian theology) is that of addressing itself not to questions of metaphysics and ontology but to questions concerning the meaning of man's historical existence. The biblical people do not, of course, suppose that man dwells in an absolutely finite province of meaning or that the human reality is self-contained and without transcendent reference; and any such histori*cism* is surely alien to the real ethos of Christian thought, for (as Ronald Gregor Smith reminds us) it is always the intention of Christian theology to address itself to what men "are not themselves": it has to do with "what they do not and never can possess at all, as part of their self-equipment or as material for their self-mastery . . . with what comes to them all the time from beyond themselves."[2] Biblical faith is, nevertheless, as we have come to see, not slanted towards ontology or metaphysics, but towards the dynamism of historical existence. As the late Carl Michalson remarked, "it is an *answer* to the question of the meaning of history where the answer is given within history *as* history and not at the horizon of history as being."[3] Though the Bible contains many statements about the cosmos, they are statements that are almost always to be seen as subservient to the basic intention of interpreting and commenting on the actualities of historical experience, on the immediacies of the life-world, for this is what the Bible wants basically to do—to

2. Ronald Gregor Smith, "A Theological Perspective of the Secular," *The Christian Scholar*, 43, no. 1 (March 1960), p. 15.
3. Carl Michalson, "Theology as Ontology and as History," in *The Later Heidegger and Theology* (1 of *New Frontiers in Theology*), ed. by James M. Robinson and John B. Cobb, Jr. (New York, Harper & Row, 1963), p. 147.

publish, to declare, to interpret "a series of events, an *oikonomia,* an *ordo salutis.*"[4]

The Dutch philosopher-theologian, Cornelis van Peursen, is recalling at a certain point in one of his recent essays the passage of the people of Israel over the Red Sea, how the east wind parted the waters and enabled them to cross over and escape their Egyptian pursuers, and how their sense of reality not only led them in effect to say, "It is the east wind" but also led them to say, "It is *He.*"[5] This incident from the Exodus-narrative does indeed very nicely suggest what is most striking in the biblical mentality, for, in the context of Israel's experience, God is not so much a Thing, a Being, to be inferred from events or to be resorted to as a principle of explanation by way of making sense of events that would otherwise be inexplicable. He is, rather—the "I am who I am"—the name given to the deepest meanings that the inspired imagination of the people locates in the events themselves, in the concrete situations of their own lives. Their historical experience is not one thing, and God then another; on the contrary, the two are but obverse sides of one reality. Though the children of Abraham are a people who have a great responsiveness to the *mysterium tremendum et fascinosum,* the Glory and the Majesty belong to a Presence which is to be encountered only in the concrete blessings and defeats, only in the actual victories and calamities, that make up the living reality of the people's sojourn on this earth.

Thus faith—that radical kind of faith which enables a man to endure all the shocks and vicissitudes of life with an ultimate nonchalance and cheerfulness and hope—for the biblical community, is not anything that belongs to a sphere above or outside the realm of time and history. For them it is not (as Gerhard Ebeling puts it) "a kind of speculative soaring into transcendence. But it determines existence as existence in this

4. Théo Preiss, *Life in Christ,* Studies in Biblical Theology, 13, trans. Harold Knight (London, S.C.M. Press, 1954), p. 66.
5. See Cornelis A. van Peursen, "Man and Reality—the History of Human Thought," *Student World,* 56, no. 1 (First Quarter 1963), p. 20.

world, and thus it is not something alongside all that I do and suffer, hope and experience, but something that is concretely present in it all, that is, it determines all my doing and suffering, hoping and experiencing."[6] In the biblical perspective on things, the "material of faith" (in Dr. Ebeling's phrase) is simply this actual world where a man must hold out against this and take a stand against that and resist whatever threatens to stain or contradict or blaspheme the Glory. The sphere of faith, in other words, is the shifting, conditioned, ambiguous site of history itself. Thus the Bible does not accord an ultimate validity to any sort of distinction between the sacred and the profane. Such a distinction is occasionally to be found bidding for Israel's suffrage, but it never manages finally to prevail, for the One in whose gracious fidelity Israel finds the hinge of her history solicits from the people of the Covenant, above all else, a true steadfastness in historical responsibility, acts of justice and charity and compassion, not any sort of abdication from the precincts of the world for the sake of attaining the security to be afforded by some pure and holy realm outside the historical continuum.

Thus it is that the central thrust of Hebraic faith is generally defined in our time by the great interpreters of biblical experience, by Gerhard von Rad, Walther Eichrodt, Otto Procksch, Martin Buber, Abraham Heschel, and numerous others.

Nor does the New Testament present an essentially different orientation. Though it may, in the occasional rigorism of its eschatology and apocalypticism, appear to be moving towards an otherworldly kind of spirituality, the ultimate norm which it invokes is by no means a transcendent datum lying beyond time and historical existence. Indeed, in one of the most stunningly brilliant essays of our generation in biblical theology, the Professor of New Testament Studies at Basel, Oscar Cullmann, argues with great power—in his book of 1946, *Christus und die Zeit* (*Christ and Time*)—that the very

6. Gerhard Ebeling, *The Nature of Faith*, trans. Ronald Gregor Smith (Philadelphia, Fortress Press, 1961), pp. 159–60.

distinction between time and eternity is something essentially alien to the deepest commitments of primitive Christianity. This characteristically Hellenic scheme, he maintains, is displaced in biblical thought by the polarity between this present age and the age to come; and "eternity" in the New Testament is nothing more than "the endless succession of the ages." Not even the advent of Christ breaches the consistent temporalism of the biblical community; it is redeemed, of course, from a purely futurist orientation to time, for the center of history is now brought out of the future and into the present age—the decisive deed of God is now descried in Jesus of Nazareth. But even in Christ time is not felt to have been invaded by something that is not time; no, says Cullmann, in Christ, time for the primitive Christian imagination has simply reached its "midpoint"—which is to say that the ultimate norm of the New Testament is an historical norm, namely, the single fact of Jesus Christ and the temporally connected series of events comprising the history of the biblical people which finds its "center" in Christ. And it is in something like Cullmann's direction that many of those comprising the avant-garde today in New Testament studies seem to be moving; in the bluntness of his denial that otherworldliness is an essential ingredient of New Testament faith, he seems to be marking out the general route being taken in one way or another by many scholars (most radically perhaps, and controversially, by the German, Herbert Braun) among that large corps that has responded to the *Entmythologisierung* program of Rudolf Bultmann.

It is this whole drift in the recent study of biblical thought that has encouraged theology to disavow those interpretations of the Christian faith that have the effect of converting it into a supernaturalistic system of metaphysical doctrine—whose cultural role then becomes simply that of still another heteronomy standing over against its competitors in the forum of contending *Weltanschauungen*, with a whip and a sword. What is bequeathed to systematic theology by the radical biblical scholarship of our period, and its drastic reconceptualization of the biblical mentality, is not (as some young theologians have misguidedly concluded) any sort of scheme for having, as it were, the Gospel without God. It is, rather, the suggestion that any theology that wants, even in the slightest degree, to remain faithful to the traditionally ultimate norm of *sola scriptura* will forswear, in its explication of the Christian message, any and every version of the old "metaphysic of distinction between the place of God and the place of man"[7] as profoundly untrue to the essential logic of biblical faith. This is not, to be sure, a faith for which belief in a transcendent God is a dispensable excrescence, but what the ablest scholars of Hebraic thought in our day have been perceiving ever more clearly over many years is that, for the people of Israel, the transcendence is always, and inseparably, related to their experience of their own history. As Gregor Smith says, it is not

> an addendum to this history, it is not excogitated from the events in such a way as to leave the events behind; nor is it imposed upon the events in such a way as to exalt the transcendence at the expense of the reality of the events. But the two are woven together in an inextricable web which is itself the one single reality for Israel. Their history is their relation with God; and God is their history.[8]

It is appropriate, in other words, to speak of that ultimate reality under which Israel and the primitive Christian community stand as the will of God, but it is for them a reality discoverable only in the concrete political and cultural situations of their lives; and, as Walther Eichrodt says, it drives them ever more deeply "into the midst of history with all its insecurity and unforeknowable possibilities."[9]

The radical implications of this biblical legacy for theological reconstruction in our period have been very sensitively

7. Ronald Gregor Smith, *The New Man: Christianity and Man's Coming of Age* (New York, Harper & Bros., 1956), p. 108.

8. Ibid., pp. 28–29.

9. Walther Eichrodt, *Man in the Old Testament*, Studies in Biblical Theology, 4, trans. K. and R. Gregor Smith (Chicago, Henry Regnery, 1951), pp. 25–26.

perceived by many of the central strategists of Christian thought at the present time—by the late Paul Tillich, by Rudolf Bultmann, by the late Friedrich Gogarten, by Gerhard Ebeling and Ernst Fuchs, and numerous others. But our generation seems more and more to feel that none has grasped the issue with such acuteness and passion as did the gifted young German theologian, Dietrich Bonhoeffer, who was martyred by Himmler's henchmen in the Bavarian forest on the 10th of April, 1945. The crucial document is, of course, that fragmentary collection of *obiter dicta* comprised of a remarkable set of notes and letters to friends—*Letters and Papers from Prison*—nearly all of which were written in Tegel Prison in Berlin between the spring of 1943 and the autumn of 1944. Here it was, amid the bleakness of a Gestapo prison cell, that this young scholar boldly undertook a fresh assessment of the whole problem of faith in relation to modern experience. What seems most to have borne in upon him, with a strange new kind of compelling force, was the realization that indeed the very essence of "religion" is profoundly incompatible with any biblically grounded faith. For the basic premise of "religion" is the old "metaphysic of distinction between the place of God and the place of man"; religion, that is, invites man to conceive himself as a point of intersection between two spheres, the natural and the supernatural, the temporal and the eternal; "the religious premise" (as Bonhoeffer called it) postulates a *terra incognita* "above" or "beyond" the place that is occupied by man, and it rests upon the notion of a *Deus ex machina* to whose "existence" that of all other beings is subordinate. But the course that his meditations took during the last months of his life led Bonhoeffer to face deeply into how impossible it has become for any man breathing the cultural atmosphere of the modern world to think of reality as an affair of two realms. For "the linchpin" of the whole structure is gone; the *Deus ex machina* is simply no longer comprehensible by the modern imagination. "We are proceeding towards a time of no religion at all: men as they are now simply cannot be religious any more,"[10] for they have "come of age," and, living amid a world characterized by the kinds of regularities described by empirical science, they can no longer find any good reason for resorting to a God of the stopgap, for supposing that the public world of normal experience is somehow completed and given a final coherence by a supernatural order.

In short, his meditation on the full meaning of the whole cultural enterprise initiated by the Renaissance and the Enlightenment led Bonhoeffer to the conclusion that the time for religion is gone, that—in the world of modern physics and biology and psychology—"the religious premise" is reduced to an irreparable debris, and man is no longer the *homo religiosus*. If God is still to be spoken of at all, it must be, he decided, in a "nonreligious" way.

But—and here is what is really decisive—"nonreligious interpretation" is not merely an apologetic maneuver required by the modern situation; it is, far more fundamentally, in Bonhoeffer's sense of things, a stratagem required by the very nature of biblical faith itself, and by the inherent logic of Christian theology. For Christian faith is not itself religion; indeed, one might imagine the formula *religio est negatio Christi* as the motto for Bonhoeffer's whole message, since, in his lexicon, religion means a system of supernaturalism, the doctrine of the two realms, the God of the stopgap, the interpretation of transcendence in metaphysical terms, the spatialization of the Divine, the projection into the skies of a heavenly *Pantokrator*, the "forcing [of] God out of the world"—and a biblically grounded faith stands as the fundamental opposite of all this. Indeed, the man who finds his basic fulcrum in such a faith will not even be too fascinated with the Transcendent, and certainly he will not cogitate upon "the plans and accom-

---

10. Dietrich Bonhoeffer, *Letters and Papers from Prison*, trans. Reginald Fuller, and ed. Eberhard Bethge (London, William Collins Sons, [Fontana Books], 1959), p. 91.

plishments of a self-existent Supreme Being"[11] for the sake of building a system of doctrine wherewith to assault that which is presumably opposed to this Being—namely, the world. So to proceed would be to have all askew the truly biblical reality which is constituted by the presence (in Bonhoeffer's phrase) of "the 'beyond' in the midst of our life"[12]—the "beyond" which is the creative ground and meaning of all our most significant social, political, and cultural experiences—where, for the biblical people, the deep things of God are to be found. Such a procedure would be a *negatio Christi*, since Christ's great vocation was not that of promoting a new religion—"neither circumcision nor uncircumcision"—but, rather, of calling men to a radical solicitude for and openness to the world. Hence, for Bonhoeffer, the vocation of the Christian man is not primarily that of being "religious" in any particular way but is that of living "a 'worldly' life," a life of the deepest engagement with the full human and cultural reality of the particular moment to which history commits him—and a life grounded in the confidence that the Holy and the Sacred are to be encountered in the true depth of that historical reality. Bonhoeffer recognized, of course, that the Bible message and the Christian faith have for countless ages worn the "garment" of religion, but the great positive advantage, he felt, which is brought by such a secular age as our own is the spur it provides to the Christian faith to cast off inessentials and to strip itself of a garment which no longer has any vitally functional validity.

So faith, in his view—that is, genuinely Christian faith—is not a matter of acceding to difficult metaphysical propositions about spooky realities; it is, rather—insofar as its posture is in conformity with Christ's—an affirmative orientation toward one's neighbor and, in our time, toward a world come of age (in the sense of no longer needing religion). Thus the Christian community, in the degree to which it truly understands

11. Helmut Gollwitzer, *The Existence of God as Confessed by Faith*, trans. James Leitch (Philadelphia, Westminster Press, 1965), p. 88.

12. Dietrich Bonhoeffer, *Letters*, p. 93.

the meaning of the biblical message and its present historical situation, will not be found prancing into the forums of our cultural life today with any metaphysical or religious baggage that has the effect of shutting it off from the characteristic intellectual vitalities of the modern period. It will instead be zealous in offering the world a "religionless" interpretation of its faith, an interpretation which forswears the old "metaphysic of distinction between the place of God and the place of man" and which gives itself wholly to an inquiry into how the human future can be responsibly faced, with confidence and prophetic hope.

This is the testimony that is bequeathed us from Bonhoeffer's cell, during the last months of his life, in Tegel Prison; and there is, of course, much that is cryptic and obscure in the *Letters and Papers from Prison*. What precisely is the nature of the hermeneutic that is to govern a nonreligious interpretation of biblical concepts and theological categories? How far can a religionless Christianity be expected to preserve the real genius of the Gospel and not to convert itself into simply another form of Ethical Culture? And what really is it that defines the doctrine of God on which a religionless Christianity rests? These and numerous other questions are raised and yet remain unanswered by the tantalizing fragments that came out of Bonhoeffer's jail between the 14th of April, 1943, and the 28th of December, 1944. But, for all of their gnomic tenuity, they have more profoundly fascinated the theological imagination of our period than any other single body of utterance. Despite the continuing prestige of Barth, Bultmann, Tillich, and the Niebuhrs, it is the Bonhoeffer of the *Prison Letters* (and to some extent of the *Ethics*, written between 1940 and 1943, but unfinished, and posthumously published in 1949) who is the great weather vane of contemporary theology. This is not, of course, to say that the *Letters and Papers from Prison* affords a simple index of a prevailing consensus, for it is itself too problematical to have established a basic program of work for theology; and what there is in it of real consistency has by no means, in all of its detail, elicited anything like universal approval. Nevertheless, there is no other single document of our period that seems so nicely to express the temper of mind that is today most pervasively characteristic of Christian theology. In his way of responding at once to the received biblical message and to the modern situation Bonhoeffer may be considered, in relation to the general effort of theology in our time, as enacting a large exemplary role; for the best theological intelligence today has long since given up being aghast at the autonomy which modern cultural enterprise lays claim to and has become convinced that the Incarnation is best honored not by derogating an autonomous secularity or by attempting to bully it into submission to some presumably sacrosanct authority of the Church's *kerygma* but, rather, by allowing the world to be itself, most especially when that world, by the sophistication of its intellectual pursuits, has won access to great maturity and has (as Bonhoeffer liked to say) "come of age." And the Word of God begins to be heard not only in the scripture, proclamation, and sacraments of the community of faith but in all those intellectual and cultural forms which, as they arise out of man's deepest encounter with his world and his own humanity, are stamped by a self-authenticating genuineness and relevance.

What begins, in other words, to be most repugnant to the newly emerging Christian sensibility is any doctrine of two realms, of a sphere to which the truth of faith belongs and, standing over against it, a sphere to which something else that is to be called "the world" belongs. The supposition that the Christian man is related to *two* realms has come to be so profoundly alien to the new ethos of theological thought primarily as a result of the repossession of what Karl Barth many years ago called "the strange new world within the Bible." What is more and more insisted upon is that "the obedient devotion of the human spirit to the objects of Christian revelation is not complete without the recognition of the freedom of the human spirit"[13] in relation to all the realities and possibilities

13. Ronald Gregor Smith, *New Man*, p. 58.

of its own history. The world, in short, is one, and the only significant difference that is established in the case of the Christian man has to do with his faith as to whence it is from which come the great gifts of courage and creativity and peace. But his role, it is felt, is surely not, as I have elsewhere remarked,

to bully the world into granting its suffrage to some special system of propositions of his own invention. For he does not come into this world from another world like a *deus ex machina*, with a marvelous formula that can unlock all the entanglements of human culture. No, he lives in the historical order like all his fellows: the resource on which he relies is simply that particular hope and confidence to which he is given access in this world by reason of what he knows God to have done for this world. And, having this resource, his single vocation is to live, as did Jesus the Lord, in solicitude for, and in openness to, the men to whom he is related by the particular moment in history in which he happens to stand.

The Christian scholar faces the same world that is faced by all other men; and . . . it is outrageous arrogance for him to assume that his faith provides him with some sort of privileged perspective by means of which he can integrate internally the various fields of culture and then assign to each its proper place in some tidily comprehensive arrangement that will be a Christian map of the modern mind.[14]

It is something like this that makes the general basis on which theology is today undertaking to reconceive its own identity and its relation to culture at large, and what is most notable is its increasing loss of interest in elaborating—in any systematic and sharply separatist way—a distinctive *speculum mentis* for the Christian man.

This, then, is how it comes to be today that any characteris-

14. Nathan A. Scott, Jr., *The Broken Center*, pp. 198–99.

tically contemporary attempt of theology at performing the act of self-definition tends itself to be the occasion for a kind of metaphoric exercise based on some version of the I-Thou figure of Martin Buber. Theology, it is more and more being said, *is* a form of "dialogue"; the language of "divinity," we are being reminded, *is* a form of "conversation"—or at least the effort to initiate a fruitful conversation between those who speak within and on behalf of the Church of Christ and those who represent the significant intellectual and cultural disciplines whereby man's self-interpretation is undertaken, in the deepest dimensions of his encounter with reality. Which is to say that the theological act occurs not only in the act whereby the truth of distinctively Christian faith is set forth and clarified but occurs also, and perhaps in certain ways even more critically, in the moment in which this particular faith is required to define and understand itself in relation to the general fund of human wisdom about what is important in man's life on this earth. The assumption that faith wants to make is that, "if Christ is truly the *Logos,* then He . . . is witnessed to in all apprehensions of truth, whether they occur within a framework of Christian concern or not,"[15] and the confession that is solicited from the Christian man, in a glad and joyous spirit, is that which was anciently enunciated, nearly two hundred years before Christ, by the Roman playwright Terence—"*Homo sum; humani nil a me alienum puto.*"

So the kind of scrupulous attention that is now given in the major centers of theological education to the humanistic and social sciences—to philosophy and psychology, to politics and sociology, even to economics and anthropology—and to the issues that they pose for Christian theology is not at all prompted by any unprincipled whoring after what is momentarily prestigious in the cultural Establishment, as a certain kind of smugly hostile secular observer may be inclined to suppose. It springs, rather, from a profound recovery of the real intention of biblical faith and from a consequent

15. Ibid., p. 200.

change in the estimate which theology makes as to what ought generally to be the response of the Christian imagination to the cultural life of our time. It springs from a deep conviction that, by its own inner logic, the Christian faith is required not only "to turn inward upon itself, asking what is authentically and ultimately its own kind of truth" but is also required "to move out into . . . 'a lover's quarrel with the world.' "[16] Athens, in short, is seen now to have a good deal to do with Jerusalem.

Certainly it is to this whole range of considerations that one must turn by way of accounting for the decision of my colleagues in the Divinity faculty of the University of Chicago in 1950 to establish as one of their basic Fields a department devoted to the study of the great forms and expressions of the literary imagination, with special emphasis being given to the literature of the modern period. What was paramount in their thinking was the realization that the great literature of our time—the canon established by such artists as Baudelaire, Dostoevski, Yeats, Kafka, Eliot, Rilke, Mann, Joyce, Faulkner, Stevens, Brecht—constitutes one of the most powerful expressions of modern intelligence, and a body of writing whose special genius it is to focalize in a remarkably vivid and startling way many of the issues that, in the nature of the case, must be very much at the center of any comprehensive theological anthropology. Indeed, it was perceived that many of the writers who have been most influential in the shaping of modern sensibility could be said to be "spiritual writers," in a sense very close to the meaning which this term is given in Catholic theology, for the drama being enacted in such texts as *The Notebooks of Malte Laurids Brigge, The Waste Land, The Castle, The Sound and the Fury, Doctor Faustus,* and the *Pisan Cantos* is essentially that of the soul's journey in search of God. So a fine opportunity seemed to be beckoning, for theology to venture into those chambers of imagery where the human spirit today, often unassisted by any of the supports of traditional faith, is radically probing anew into issues

16. Roger Hazelton, *New Accents in Contemporary Theology* (New York, Harper & Bros., 1960), pp. 11–12.

of ultimate import with which it is also perennially the office
of religion to deal, and doing so in a way so spirited and original as to have frequently the effect of helping faith toward a
deeper apprehension at once of itself and of the larger scene
in our age to which it wants to speak. Thus it was that the
Divinity School at Chicago was persuaded, in the autumn of
1950, to bring into existence a program of study in Theology
and Literature leading to the M.A. and the Ph.D.[17]

It remains to be remarked, however, that the customary
definition of how theology itself may be fecundated by literary study, though it has an undoubted validity, does tend to
leave certain things out of account. What is usually said is

17. In terms of curriculum, the establishment of this program was
and remains one of the most significant recent innovations in American
theological education, and continues, in the elaborateness of its effort,
to be virtually without parallel. Important work is no doubt being done
in this general area in other theological faculties, but nowhere else is
so elaborately designed a program of interdisciplinary work in theology
and criticism being conducted at the doctoral level. The various dimensions which are naturally a part of the total enterprise necessarily make
a doctorate in the field an exceedingly arduous degree, for not only
must the candidate acquire the linguistic resources that are usually a
prerequisite for the Ph.D. and not only must he (in the Divinity School's
system) survive a battery of stiff comprehensive examinations in the
basic theological disciplines (biblical studies, church history, systematic
and historical theology, etc.), but he must also, before undertaking his
research, sit for rather grueling Field Examinations (both written and
oral) in literary history and criticism and aesthetics and theology of
culture—and he must in these examinations demonstrate that he is able,
with real urbanity and sophistication, to think about the fundamental
issues of literary scholarship *as a theologian.* So, given the extensive
work that must be done at once in the Divinity School and in the
University's Division of the Humanities (in the various departments
of literature), it is a rather expensive degree and, as a consequence, no
great flood of alumni has been released into the academic marketplace.
But a dozen men, to date, have taken the doctorate; another fifteen or
more are now at the point of having very nearly completed their studies, and a much larger number are at a less advanced stage; nearly fifty
M.A.'s have been awarded; and many of these persons are beginning
already to have bright and productive careers as publishing scholars
and as teachers (in both theological and literary faculties), and are beginning to provide helpful leadership of thought in the theological
community at large as it attempts more deeply to encounter what is
prophetic in the great literature of our time.

that the literary imagination offers a peculiarly direct access to those deep interiorities of feeling that constitute a people's basic life-world. It is a kind of barometer that registers the deep currents of sensibility which give to a culture its distinctive tone and style; it brings to light what is inaccessible to the procedures of empirical study; it mirrors the age, in the subtlest nuances of its fears and aspirations, of its dreams and myths, of its hopes and nightmares. And thus, it is argued, the Christian enterprise, as it seeks to make contact with the living reality of its human environment, may find in literary art a most helpful resource. Art is viewed, in other words, in its capacity to document the Time-spirit, and, in this way, it is thought to offer churchmen an indispensable kind of index to the actual world to which the Christian Evangel is to be addressed. Such an estimate of the cultural function of art—which descends from the German Romantics of the eighteenth century, from Herder and the Schlegels, with whom *Geistesgeschichte* theory has its real beginning—though for various reasons it is today sometimes questioned—has still a certain utility, in the degree to which it encourages alertness to the integral relationships between the arts and the generality of human experience. Goethe's *Werther*, for example, does no doubt attest to a deep inflammation of sensibility that at a certain point overtook that phase of the European mind which, in following the lines of Rousseau's rebellion against eighteenth-century rationalism and in tending to make a virtual religion of feeling, found its feelings after a time to be riotously exacerbated and tyrannical and intolerably raw. Or Tennyson's *In Memoriam* surely gives, in part, a poignant expression to the astonished sense that many of the most sensitive Victorian people had—as a result of the inrush of the new biology and the new Higher Criticism—of all the traditional supports and consolations of Christian belief having suddenly been converted into a huge, nagging question mark. Or, again, in an age that has experienced the obscenity of Auschwitz and the hell of modern global warfare and the new *anomie* that is bred by the mechanisms of social life in an advanced technocratic culture, the profound dispiritedness and *apatheia* of the protagonist in Camus' *The Stranger* do very probably express a sentiment which is recurrently epidemic in our time. And, undoubtedly, a theology uninformed by that rendering which the literary imagination gives of what we call the Human Condition is not likely to speak with power and cogency, or with any real brilliance of perception.

I should like to suggest in conclusion, however, that this customary rationale for the transaction between theology and literature does to some extent fail of the necessary completeness. What needs to be kept in view is that the literary imagination may not only help theology to take a closer reading of cultural reality than it might achieve without such assistance, but it can also perform an important propaedeutic function in the quest of Christian theology for deepening of its own self-knowledge.

T. S. Eliot, it is true, bluntly denied many years ago that the imaginative writer does anything that could be called *thinking*. In his famous essay of 1927 on "Shakespeare and the Stoicism of Seneca" he said, "I can see no reason for believing that either Dante or Shakespeare did any thinking on his own. The people who think that Shakespeare thought, are always people who are not engaged in writing poetry, but who are engaged in thinking, and we all like to think that great men were like ourselves."[18] This is, I believe, a dictum which, if rigorously parsed, will yield some bit of foolishness; for to deny any "thought" to the kind of reflection that went into the making of Valéry's *Monsieur Teste*, Mann's *The Magic Mountain*, Stevens' *Harmonium*, or Eliot's own *Quartets* is surely, to an absurd extent, to suppose in effect that "thinking" must necessarily entail nothing more than a purely logical operation—and this is to deliver thought over into "the rationalist trap from which it is likely to emerge as a cripple, full of animosity against that other deformed creature,

18. T. S. Eliot, *Selected Essays: 1917–1932* (New York, Harcourt, Brace, 1932), p. 116.

mutilated in the same operation: the Romantic emotion."[19] But the real intent of Eliot's tartness on this occasion was, I take it, to assert, if somewhat obliquely, that the modalities of literary art are not, characteristically, distinguished by the systematic discursiveness belonging to formal dialectical discourse. And indeed they are not: for, drenched in "ideas" as such a poem as *Burnt Norton* manifestly is, it yet cannot be merely reduced to a doctrinal statement, because the poem is a collaboration between certain ideas, rhythms, and dramatic gestures; the poem *qua* poem, in other words, is a structure of song and statement, of rhythm and vision, that cannot be rendered, exhaustively and without remainder, in the terms of any simple argument of a univocal sort—and far more even must this be acknowledged as true of those forms of literature in which systematic ideas do not play so large a role in the poetic economy as they do in Eliot's own poetry. So, given the intransigently nondiscursive quality of literary art, how, it may be wondered, can it be conceived as capable of helping such a technical science as theology towards a larger measure of inner clarity?

Here, the answer is, I think, to be found in the fact—if I may employ an ugly neologism invented by the English philosopher R. M. Hare—that no important work of literary art is without its *blik*. This is a term which Mr. Hare has contrived for the sake of specifying what it is that theological discourse is "about." Like most contemporary philosophers, he is unwilling to grant that theological propositions might be about any existing "state of affairs"; yet he does not want to conclude that they are, therefore, meaningless. No, he says, despite their empirical unverifiability, they may be adjudged meaningful, in so far as they can be found to be expressions or affirmations of a *blik*—that is, a fundamental attitude or orientation toward the world, a basic presupposition about the meaning of experience that is not itself a consequence of empirical inquiry but which affords a standpoint from which

---

19. Erich Heller, *The Disinherited Mind*, p. 121.

experience may be ordered and interpreted.[20] Now, without setting forth any judgment as to the propriety of Mr. Hare's notion in the field of theological semantics—though my inclination is to feel that, there, in the use he makes of it, it is quite wrongheaded—I should like to take it over into the field of literary theory, for in this region of things certainly much of what gives interest to the individual poem or novel is an affair of the *blik* that is being expressed. Here, of course, there is no abstract doctrinal scheme involved; there is the same resistance to discursive translation that Mr. Hare claims to find in the *blik* of religious faith—and all depends on the vivaciousness with which a given perspective is fleshed out and dramatized through a vibrant pattern of living images, on the extent to which (as Henry James liked to say) it is fully *rendered*. Nevertheless, the poem—by which I mean the work of verbal art—is, as Cleanth Brooks puts it, "a portion of reality as viewed and valued by a human being. It is rendered coherent through a perspective of valuing."[21] This perspective is not, of course, systematically elaborated or analyzed, for what the poem wants to do is to convey, as it were, what it *feels* like to hold a given perspective, and what the existential consequences are in which the holding of it eventuates. Thus Northrop Frye suggests, very acutely, that literature bears something of the same relationship to theology that mathematics bears to the physical sciences. "The pure mathematician," he says, "proceeds by making postulates and assumptions and seeing what comes out of them, and what the poet or novelist does is rather similar."[22] For just as "pure mathematics enters into and gives form to the physical sciences," so too

20. See R. M. Hare, "Theology and Falsification," in *New Essays in Philosophical Theology*, ed. Antony Flew and Alasdair MacIntyre (London, S.C.M. Press, 1955), pp. 99–103.

21. Cleanth Brooks, "Implications of an Organic Theory of Poetry," in *Literature and Belief*, ed. M. H. Abrams (New York, Columbia University Press, 1958), p. 68.

22. Northrop Frye, *The Educated Imagination* (Bloomington, Indiana University Press, 1964), p. 127.

is it an office of the literary imagination to vitalize meditation on matters of ultimate concern by making concrete before the immediate gaze of the mind the real cost of a given life-orientation. It does not "line up arguments facing each other like football teams,"[23] but, rather—in the terms of drama and symbolic action—it *dances-out* (as Kenneth Burke would say) the real entailments of "religiousness A" and "religiousness B"; and thus it can be considered to be perhaps a radically *experimental* theology, dwelling (like pure mathematics) on the postulatory side of what formal theology (like the physical sciences) addresses itself to in its existential dimension.

The great danger always is, of course, that formal theology will become something merely formal, and thus humanly superficial and irrelevant, that it (like any science of human existence) will fall into some version of what Whitehead called the Fallacy of Misplaced Concreteness, reifying its categories into a stiff sort of punctilio that is without any genuine relevance to the living actualities of human existence. So its own health very greatly requires the quickening and enrichment that come from the kind of experimental theology that literature can be, for the novelist and the dramatist and the poet can help the theological imagination to *see* how this or that particular faith or life-orientation really *looks*, under the full stress of experience. And apart from such experimental knowledge—which the artist is uniquely empowered to convey —the work of the theologian is likely to become an arid business of syllogism and logic-chopping, and theology is likely not to win that sharp awareness of its own variousness and breadth of possibility which imaginative literature can give.

So its attentiveness to the arts of the word, as we now begin to see, may help to guarantee for the theological enterprise a strength and suppleness of intelligence that are not so surely to be won through any of the various transactions which it must undertake with other departments of culture. And thus it comes to be, increasingly, that both the seminaries of the

23. Ibid., p. 126.

The Place of Litterae Humaniores

Church and the divinity faculties of our major universities are reserving an important place for the study of literary art, not only because the work of the poet is itself addressed to the experiential material of which theology speaks and thus invites theological assessment but also because the theological imagination itself, for its own health, is found to need a literary critique. It is an interesting development, and one which promises for Christian theology today a very great deepening of its entry into the mind of our time.

Index

Index

171

Index